'The world needs more people like Dylan. This is such an important book, it's what I needed as a young person.'
Hugh van Cuylenburg

'One of life's great pleasures is to have a yarn to Dylan. After reading this book, everyone can feel like they've had one with him, too. Warm, insightful and funny. Just like Dylan.'
Tony Armstrong

'Raw, relatable and thought-provoking. Dyl's vulnerability mixed with his charming sense of humour makes this book hard to put down. Grateful to know him.'
Nedd Brockmann

'One of the best podcasts has now turned into an entertaining and insightful book. The better Dylan is showing me up again.'
Dylan Alcott AO

For my son, Max – be good to your mother.

And for those who got a Dyl & Friends *tattoo over the journey. You know who you are . . . ILY xx*

Dylan Buckley

Honest Chat

How to tackle your feelings and befriend vulnerability

VIKING
an imprint of
PENGUIN BOOKS

VIKING

UK | USA | Canada | Ireland | Australia
India | New Zealand | South Africa | China

Viking is part of the Penguin Random House group of companies whose addresses can be found at global.penguinrandomhouse.com

First published by Viking in 2023

Copyright © Dylan Buckley 2023

The moral right of the author has been asserted.

All rights reserved. No part of this publication may be reproduced, published, performed in public or communicated to the public in any form or by any means without prior written permission from Penguin Random House Australia Pty Ltd or its authorised licensees.

The information in this book is provided for general purposes only and does not take into account your personal situation, objectives or needs. Before acting on any of this information, you should consider its appropriateness to your own situation, objectives and needs and seek advice from qualified professionals in relevant areas such as health, medical and/or business.

Cover design by SODAA © Penguin Random House Australia Pty Ltd
Typeset in 11.8/18 pt Sabon by Midland Typesetters, Australia

Printed and bound in Australia by Griffin Press, an accredited
ISO AS/NZS 14001 Environmental Management Systems printer

A catalogue record for this book is available from the National Library of Australia

ISBN 978 1 76134 080 2

penguin.com.au

We at Penguin Random House Australia acknowledge that Aboriginal and Torres Strait Islander peoples are the Traditional Custodians and the first storytellers of the lands on which we live and work. We honour Aboriginal and Torres Strait Islander peoples' continuous connection to Country, waters, skies and communities. We celebrate Aboriginal and Torres Strait Islander stories, traditions and living cultures; and we pay our respects to Elders past and present.

CONTENTS

INTRODUCTION

Hey guys, Dylan Buckley here. My friends call me Dyl, so feel free to call me that if you like. I'm always happy to make new friends. And now that we're mates, I want to talk to you about my feelings.

Still here? Good stuff. You're already doing a shitload better than I would have been a few years ago. Back then, I would have been terrified to talk about my feelings in public – even though I've always loved a chat. That's because I didn't think 'real talk' was something guys did. I was a bit stuck in a certain idea of how a bloke should be.

Then one night, about five years ago, I was watching TV and stumbled on a show called *Man Up*,[1] about these physically grown but emotionally immature men learning how to be responsible. This guy on the telly, Tom Harkin, was talking about his job – going to schools and tradie work sites to talk to the guys there about their mental health and challenging traditional male stereotypes.

I was 25. And although I'd been an AFL footy player for about six years and had sat through dozens of meetings on 'resilience' and 'mindset' (most of which I'd tuned out), something about seeing it talked about on TV was different. This was the first time I'd really seen men's emotional health being spoken about so openly. They talked about how the model of the classic 'Australian Bloke' was deeply cooked and set us up for a life of never actually talking about our feelings. Which got me thinking about my life and the conversations I was avoiding and the problems that had built up because of that.

About halfway through the show, I burst into tears. *Fuck,* I realised, *I'm one of these kids. I've never had the chance to talk about my feelings.*

It hit me like a ton of bricks. Watching these grizzled old blokes on the TV, I could see elements of myself and echoes of my dad and the men of his generation – hardened old guys that go through life without ever learning about mental health or being open with their feelings. Just incredibly tough and emotionally inflexible, like Batman – you'd have to throw them off the bloody roof before you could get them to cry. When things are tough, they go to the pub and drink and banter with their mates, but never actually communicate beyond the surface level. Very stoic, they never express their emotions, except for the few that traditional masculinity allow: you can get mad, you can get frustrated, you can get drunk. But that's it. Feeling *real* sorrow or joy is a step too far.

Dad was a footy player and so was I. If you're a footy fan, you might know me from there, but if not, no worries. (Actually, since we're getting honest, I'd probably prefer it that way.) Whether you're into footy or not won't make a difference. This book isn't going to be all about footy. It's mostly just about being a guy: what that means and how we do it, and maybe, how we can be better at it. Or at least, what I've learned about being better at it. Some of the things we'll talk about might surprise you. I know they surprised me.

These days, more people know me for my podcasting career than my AFL career which, at 41 games and 18 goals over 8 years, was quietly unspectacular. You could almost dismiss it entirely, I suppose, except that without it, I wouldn't be where I am today. I won't say I failed at footy, exactly, but let's just say that by proving myself a less-than-champion footy player, I took the long way around into a life I truly love. Now I'm a professional podcaster, a keen advocate for better communication and mental health and an optimistic golfer. Today, my podcast *Dyl & Friends* is known for being a space where guests come on and speak honestly, openly and vulnerably.

A while ago, I got this message that made me cry – still makes me cry when I think about it. This young guy messaged me to tell me that he used to feel alone because he had this group of friends he just didn't align with. He was sensitive and curious and he cried when he was upset – you know, everything that's not 'traditional male behaviour'. But when he listened to my show it helped him because it felt like I was his mate and that he'd joined a group of people who wanted to live good lives and get the best out of themselves. Which gutted me in the best possible way. Because I'm exactly the same.

There are a lot of people out there like that, especially in my world – sports and other very male-oriented environments – who want to be vulnerable and emotionally healthier and stronger, but don't know where to start. I was never really good at school in terms of textbook learning and whatnot, but what got me through was finding the right person to help me when I had a problem. Looking back, I think that's probably the biggest skill a young guy can have: knowing how and when to ask for help and being able to identify the right person to help them over a particular hurdle. Working that out was the starting point for everything, for me: the life I've built, the people I surround myself with, the podcasts I make and this book I'm writing – the one you're now holding.

The other day, my mate Nick, who works with me in the studio and is somewhat of a mentor, hit me right in the brain when he told me, 'The best advice I've ever been given is: "Make yourself able to take advice from anyone."' That floored me. I think it was just a passing comment from Nick, but I hit him up about it later because it's probably the wisest thing I've ever heard. He'll often say something that knocks the wind out of me because it's so spot-on and nails what I'm trying to get my head around. In this case: *Everyone has something to offer – even people who you don't get along with, even people who are objectively dickheads. Everyone has a lesson for you.*

If you open yourself up and really listen, you never know what you're going to find. I'm so blessed and grateful that my job is literally that. Podcasting gives me so much, but maybe the best part is the chance to meet and pick the brains of the most amazing people – the little nuggets of wisdom you absorb from listening to others. So, that's what this book is going for. *This* story, the one you're reading right now, will give you some of my journey and some of those big lessons I've learned along the way. And sorry, I know that this word gets thrown around a lot, but it really is a journey. Life starts, then it ends – and what happens in between is up to us and how much we're willing to learn. Basically, it boils down to one really simple thing: we don't have the answers to every question, not even *half* the questions we ask ourselves on a daily basis. But someone out there does.

This book is a collection of things that have helped get me over my own obstacles – things I've learned first-hand and from others. A big disclaimer: these are what worked for me. Some of them might work for you, some of them probably won't. The only thing I can say 100 per cent is: keep an open mind as you go. There's no big life lesson, but there are so, so many teachers along the way – little moments that can help you shift direction and attitude.

Figuring out how to make life work for you is basically what this book's about. Through it, I'll share some chats I've had with a bunch of great people – Tom and many others – and a bunch of tools that have worked for me, so you can test them out for yourself and see if any work for you too. This isn't the kind of book that's heavy. Just some gems of honest chats.

I'm not much of a reader myself, truthfully, so I've tried to pull it together in a way that you can dip into and out of it, however and whenever it suits you. Read it all at once, or read it in fits and spurts; from front to back, or random sections when you're in the mood. Me, I like to read with a highlighter handy. That way, if anything strikes me in the moment I can give it some extra attention – a reminder that this is something to come back to.

This book is a way for me to pass on the nuggets I've been given. There's so much to get from life and if you open yourself up to learning and real connection with others then you've got an amazing journey ahead of you.

Let's go.

IDENTITY

CHAPTER 1

THE HARDEST THING

Honestly, the hardest thing I've ever done was to have a chat. Truly. No physical discomfort has even *come close* to the difficulty level of this particular chat. I've been frozen, tackled, knocked out, snapped this bone and that tendon, all in the pursuit of footy glory and *none* of it compared to how hard it was to sit down and say what I needed to:

'Dad, I'm worried about you. Your drinking is out of control. I think you're an alcoholic.'

It was honest and it was confronting. Real talk between two men. Now, it had been a bit of a slog for me to get to this point (which we'll get into a bit later) because, typically, I didn't have these sorts of chats with my dad. Footy blokes don't do that. Typically, footy blokes have a banter, rib each other to death, train hard, play hard and never bloody whinge. I know. I grew up in a legendary Carlton household where this traditional model of Aussie manhood was on full display.

See, my dad, Jim Buckley, was Carlton's centreman/ on-baller for 15 seasons during the late 70s and 80s – the Blues team with a reputation for being hard-training, hard-playing and hard-partying. They won three flags in four years and their weekly celebrations were legendary. During Dad's long but injury-struck career he played 164 games and scored 146 goals, then went on to coach country and suburban teams.

Dad is the best of blokes and the best of dads and around Princes Park, a deadset legend. I love my dad, but *everybody* loves my dad. Growing up, I thought that's just how it was, that everybody's dad was a famous footy player. It wasn't until embarrassingly late that the penny dropped that my dad was a big deal back in the day. I remember, as a young tyke, walking into a Carlton event with Dad and seeing all the heads whip around like, 'There's Jim Buckley's son, Dylan.' So, it was probably always on the cards that I was going to play footy. I guess you could say it runs in the family.

Growing up, most of my childhood was close enough to Princes Park (home of the Carlton Blues) to hear the siren calling and when I was old enough, I went out to meet it. I kicked my first Sherrin when I was around six years old, but I'll say right up front, my old man never ever put pressure on me to play. Mum and Dad were pretty proud of me when I became a footy player, and later on, they were proud when I stopped. I'm sure if I'd never played a game they wouldn't have loved me any less. The only thing that's ever mattered to them is that I'm happy. So, going into footy was my choice. I wanted to make them proud, but that was about the extent of them influencing my decision.

Did I feel the pressure of legacy? Not at all. Did I have a love for the game? Absolutely. In 2007 I played in the Under-15s and made the Victorian team, which was a pretty big achievement for that age. The next year I became captain of the Under-16s and from there made the 2009 Australian Institute of Sport Australian Football League (AIS–AFL) team, which travelled and played internationally for Australia. In 2010 I represented Vic Metro in the AFL Under-18 Championships. Those games are one of the main pathways towards being drafted into the professional league, so from there I sort of knew I was going to go pro.

I was a promising recruit – fast, hungry – and came with a sort of pedigree as Jim Buckley's son. At least, that's how the AFL saw it. There's nothing footy loves more than a good footy dynasty story; there's even a special father–son rule that allows teams to skip the queue when recruiting a star player's offspring. As footy stories go, the only thing better than a legendary player is the son of a legendary player taking on the crown – provided the crown fits. Which it never quite did for me, despite my actual forehead having a good amount of real estate where it might have rested.

Greater Western Sydney (GWS) Giants had an option to call shotgun on a certain number of 17-year-old players before they turned 18 (and officially eligible for the draft) and there was some speculation they would make me an offer. Before they could, Carlton recruited me under the father–son rule. In April 2010, as I was about to head overseas on an AIS–AFL South African tour, Carlton approached me with an offer. After some discussions and a handshake, it was done. I was officially a pro AFL footballer.

It was the start of Year 11. At an age where most boys are still figuring out what they want to do with the rest of their lives, my future was more-or-less in the bag. I cruised through my final year of school knowing I'd walk straight out of my school uniform into a Carlton guernsey and an AFL career – and all the profile, money and glory that comes with it.

It was the worst thing that ever happened to me.

Being handed this perfect life on a plate somehow gave me the idea that life would be easy. I happily threw all my eggs into that one basket and embraced my future. *No worries, that's all sorted then*. From then on, I didn't try at school and didn't even really try to better myself at footy.

I guess I took it for granted, which is the worst thing anyone can do with an opportunity of that magnitude. Most guys – probably 90 per cent of pro-level draft prospects – don't know if they're going to get picked up. Accordingly, they work their arses off. They've got to go to the draft and spend that Under-18 year absolutely trying their heart out to get picked up – then at the end of the year, find out if they've made it.

I already knew I had a guernsey. By chance, number 16, which my dad had worn all through his Blues' career, had recently become available and it was offered to me – a huge honour, obviously. But I declined and chose a new one: number 7. I was determined to make my own mark on the game, to be my own man. But determination only works if you're hungry and I wasn't nearly hungry enough to do what the job called for.

Here's a story that really sums up my attitude. I was touring with the Under-16s and we were out at Blacktown in Western Sydney for a footy carnival to promote AFL. As part of it, some Sydney Swans came to meet the young players. We were in this meeting room and Adam Goodes came out. Here was this absolute legend, with couple of flags under his belt, dual Brownlow medals, an icon on and off the field, giving us a bit of the old motivational speech: put in the effort, believe in yourself, work hard and you could become champions and one day win a premiership flag.

And I was listening, thinking, *Yeah, that's me. 100 per cent. I can't wait for this.*

Then another player stood up, about my height, and introduced himself.

'I'm Kieren Jack.'

Who the fuck is Kieren Jack? I'm thinking, because I don't know this guy at all. And I was a footy obsessive. I knew every player at every club, guernseys, stats, all of it, and I'd never heard of him. He must have just been drafted, but he wasn't short of confidence.

'I've just transitioned over from rugby. And I'm really looking forward to debuting for the Swans,' he said, then added, 'And one day I'm going to be captain.'

Incredulous is the word I reckon I'd use to describe how I took that. I looked at the man, all quiet confidence, and was like, *Who does this guy think he is? No chance, like, he's literally gonna be there for a couple of years. Probably just ticking a box because the Swans need a reserve.*

With the benefit of hindsight, I'm happy to admit I was mistaken. Kieren Jack ended up as co-captain, replacing Adam Goodes when he stepped down in 2013. Over his career, Kieran played 256 games and kicked 166 goals – just a couple more than me then, fair play. He really wanted it and did what it took to get there.

Kieren was hungry in a way I wasn't. I didn't think I needed to worry about my future because I thought I'd already made it. Because there was this path in front of me I thought I'd just rock up, play 300 games, win a few premierships, maybe a Brownlow, and then retire happy. None of that could be further from the truth.

Waiting room

My AFL career didn't exactly see me bolt out of the gates. After missing the recruits' training pathway because I'd got listed while still at school, I broke my ankle in my Under-18s draft year and had to have the rest of the season off. The club didn't want to rush me back onto the field, instead told me to take some time, recover, and get my ankle ready for my big debut the following year.

At the time, I was fine with it. Looking back, I should have tried to get back on field the minute I could and keep playing, but I took the club's word and took the year off. I thought my natural-born talent would see me cruise through, so I was happy to wait.

Eventually, I made my debut in Round 3 of the 2013 season, starting as a substitute. It was a warm night at Etihad Stadium (now Marvel Stadium) down in Docklands, the Saturday game against Geelong in front of a 43,000-strong crowd. We suffered a blow in the first quarter when Matthew Kreuzer broke a thumb on the field, so I was called into play much earlier than anticipated.

If you'll let me pump my own tyres a bit, I came out strong. After less than a minute of play, I swooped on the ball deep in the left-forward pocket, turned for a beautiful left-foot snap, and scored a goal – my first ever pro-AFL kick. I finished the game with five disposals, a respectable result, and was stoked.

But that was my only game for that year. We ended up losing to Geelong by 16 points and after that one taste of action, I was sent back to the reserves. Later that year, I hurt my shoulder and didn't get another opportunity at senior level until late in the 2014 season. From there, I kept racking up injuries and found myself on the sidelines more and more often.

The view from the bench

I had some bad luck, injuries-wise, but I wouldn't harp on about that too much. It's just part of footy, unfortunately. For such a short career, I collected quite a few knocks: surgeries on my left hand, my wrist broken in four places, both shoulders, left Achilles' tendinopathy, left ankle, right knee, repetitive calf strains and my back. My back was probably the worst. Over the years I've had really bad disk slips in my back which were quite debilitating for a while. But a lot of guys deal with a lot of injuries. It's the work part of playing the game – you get hurt, you throw yourself into rehab and recovery, you come back strong. So, honestly, injuries were not the problem. I think for me, the biggest hindrance was myself. The fact that I played no games in my first season and only one in the second, and I was pretty rapt with that result? That's not the mindset of a real AFL player. And it took me a long time to work that out.

That's not the mindset of a real AFL player. And it took me a long time to work that out.

Let me paint a quick picture of my attitude that first year at Carlton, where I was swapping in and out of the seniors and VFL interchange. Theoretically, I should have improved steadily, rising to the occasions presented and moving towards a permanent spot in the big league. Instead, my performance was wildly inconsistent. One game I'd kick four goals and the next, literally never touch the ball. I remember after one game out at Box Hill – in which I'd had two touches, total – our coach came up to me afterwards.

'What,' he wanted to know, 'are you doing?'

'Oh, mate, you know, I just . . . dunno what happened,' I said.

'No,' he said. 'What are you doing?'

I didn't know what to say to that, so in the end sort of mumbled, 'I honestly don't, like . . . I'm not sure.'

'Yeah. Yeah right,' he said, and just walked off shaking his head.

Which, looking back, was a clear wakeup call. One that I ignored. One of many that I ignored. Because, frankly, I was embarrassed. I'd never faced any feedback before and didn't know how to handle it. I look back to that age and cringe now at my lack of awareness and understanding of what it meant to be great. My coaches and other leaders at the Blues did their best, but eventually they stopped trying to give me advice.

'We're not actually gonna give you feedback anymore,' one coach told me. 'You don't take it on board. You think you know everything.'

But I'd always been like that. Supremely confident in my abilities. Or at least I used to think that way, back in the beginning.

In all honesty, I was probably playing my best footy from the ages of 15 to 17. That's when I was the most motivated, most driven and before other factors did me in. The footy I played then was what made the AFL recruiters notice me in the first place. I wanted to succeed when I was a young gun, but when I actually got to the AFL, I thought that I'd made it. I lost the magic that actually got me there.

It's not that I stopped giving it my all. I gave everything I thought I had in the tank. But there was so much more I could have been giving; I was only tapping my potential, not unleashing it. So, what was holding me back? The answer came to me later on and it wasn't an easy thing to come to terms with. The only thing holding me back was me.

Negativity is a magnet

In 2016, Brendon 'Bolts' Bolton came in as the coach of Carlton. Bolts was one of a kind, an incredibly elite thinker of the game. He's one of the most switched-on units I've ever met in my life. I've never seen anything like it. Probably a little bit too switched on for me if I'm honest. That's probably why it didn't work out too well – I was overthinking everything already and Bolts saw every angle.

While 2015 had been a fairly ordinary year for the Blues, personally I'd had a really good season, playing 18 games, kicking five goals, and playing a career-high game against Fremantle in Round 16. When Bolts came in he wanted to change things up across the team, moving me from the midfield – where I was playing what I thought was my best game – to try me out in different spots on the field. I wasn't having any of it. Under Heath Scotland's mentorship I was starting to feel more confident in the backline and was playing quite aggressively, getting the ball forward on the field, getting results. The way I saw it, I was doing so well on defence it seemed crazy to move me anywhere else. So I didn't embrace that opportunity, which inevitably led to some tension between me and the team.

The next two years were probably the weirdest and worst in terms of my psychological state. I'd gotten it into my head that the whole world was against me. That everyone who was trying to get me to improve myself had it in for me. My mindset was so negative I'd started to externalise everything I was doing wrong. If I had a bad game or missed a goal it was always the coach's fault, or another player's. In my mind, it had nothing to do with me. Everything I did poorly was everyone else's problem.

Because I couldn't take feedback, I'd turned down an opportunity to move into a new position and evolve my style of play. If I'd been thinking more clearly, I would have recognised that these coaching decisions I didn't understand were opportunities to embrace a new type of footy. Instead of making that leap, I just shut down. Which meant my footy suffered. And with my footy in the toilet, I was rarely being sent out on game night. That meant spending a lot of time off-field feeling sorry for myself. I kept having the same conversations with the same five guys, all sitting in the twos (reserves), all knowing we were probably not going to be there in the AFL next year, all because we felt the team was being run into the ground.

It all came to a head in one pivotal moment. It was towards the end of my career – after my 2015 breakout, my footy going downhill ever since – when I got pulled into a meeting with the coach. I'd been trying to avoid Bolts because I just didn't want to deal with him. Deep down, I blamed him for my poor form on field and couldn't be fucked talking to him. I turned up and sat down, full of attitude.

'How do you think the club's going?' he asked me.

'Oh yeah, it's going alright.'

'No, no,' he said, leaning forward. 'Tell me. How do *you* think it's going?'

And I decided, *You know what, I'm going to fucking let this guy have it. I'm really going to tell him what I think.* I went at him.

'You know what mate? It's going pretty shit,' I told him. 'Everyone's pissed off. A lot of the players aren't getting a look in. You're playing all the young guys. You're not giving us games. You should know, there's bad culture and all the players are unhappy . . .' and so on. I gave him both barrels.

Bolts sat back quietly and listened. Then asked me, very calmly, 'Who's saying these things?'

'Lots of . . . just the players. I'm not throwing anyone under the bus.'

'You don't have to tell me names. But just think in your head – who's saying those things?'

I sat, arms folded.

'Is the captain saying that? Is Patrick Cripps?' he asked, name-checking one of our rising stars who would later go on to win the 2022 Brownlow.

People who complain only complain to people they know are going to agree with them.

'No, Cripps isn't saying that.'

'Dylan, you are hanging around with the wrong people,' he said very calmly. 'Because people who complain only complain to people they know are going to agree with them.'

I remember that moment so clearly. I felt winded, like I'd been punched right in the solar plexus. Bolts had brought me into this meeting where I'd gone in all righteous, thinking I was going to own him, and instead, he'd done this sort of emotional judo throw on me. Without using any force, or raising his voice, or throwing his weight around, he made me see that *I was the problem* with the whole situation. That I was the negative one.

I saw that I'd been letting the situation control me instead of controlling the one thing I could: my attitude. Then, making it ten times worse by whinging to anyone who'd agree with me. Bolts was right – I hadn't gone to the captain with my issues because he had a winner's mindset and, subconsciously, I knew he wouldn't put up with my bullshit.

Looking back, this was the first step to the very different approach I use these days whenever things start going sideways. Knowing that the only thing we ever *really* have control of is our reaction, I use it to flip the switch. Changing it can make all the difference. This realisation was a real lightbulb moment. From then on a lot of things started to change in my life. It was a turning point in a really challenging year.

It was also bittersweet because I'd finally begun to work out some important things about life. Because my footy wasn't going so well, I'd had to start focusing on something bigger than my career – becoming a better person. I had clarity – not yet on what to do with my life, but at least on what sort of person I wanted to become. I'd begun to develop more of an intentional mindset. *I've got a choice to be positive, it's a choice to be a good guy. Good things will come if you can see the lighter side of things.*

It didn't turn my fortunes on the field around, but it was the start of a journey for me.

Have a cry, why don't ya? Really, go ahead, it feels awesome

It sounds strange to admit, but the fact I'd never really experienced adversity was hugely detrimental. I'd reached adulthood without ever having had anything bad happen to me. I'd gotten everything I'd ever wanted. Every team I'd gone after, I gotten into. Anything I'd wanted to do, I'd done. I had never experienced someone saying 'No,' or 'You can't do that.'

It wasn't necessarily arrogance, I just think that being a young guy, if things are going well, your ego can creep up on you and you don't even realise it. That was definitely the case for me. For my first years in the guernsey, I just didn't get it. In all honesty, I have no one to blame for missing games but myself. I didn't really know what hard work was. I was so young and had no idea of what it took to improve. So I did the worst possible thing a young player can do: I became complacent.

As time passed and the reality of my career played out, it started to become increasingly obvious that my identity was going one way and my footy the other. I could no longer believe in myself as a 'champion player'. When looking at my game stats versus the guy in the mirror, it was clear that my identity was falling apart in real time. And honestly, it hurt.

Truth is, I had a bit of an ego – which is fine; a healthy ego is part of what keeps you safe and mentally healthy. Ego protects your sense of self and identity and helps you overcome adversity. But human beings, and in particular young males, aren't always well-equipped to respond to stress on the ego. On a biological level, brain scans show that the same area of the brain is activated both when your identity is being threatened and when you are being physically attacked.[2] So basically, when your ego is under attack, it feels like a real threat, something you have to fight against.

That becomes extra complicated in our culture where young males aren't encouraged to be vulnerable or sensitive or communicate with their partner or mates on a deeper level. Let me ask you this: when you see a young guy crying, is your first instinct to reach out and help, or do you think, *Oh, he's having a sook*, or *He's weak* and give him shit about it?

I know what the usual is, 'cause for a long time that was me. But let me tell you what I've learned . . . When we judge crying as weakness, that's us acting badly from fear of our own vulnerability. Guys find crying terrifying because it challenges our identity. But here's something else I've learned. Crying is healthy. I fucking love crying. I've cried five times today. Healthy masculinity is the opposite of being stoic and emotionally shut down.

Soften the fuck up, mate

I think the moment you start dropping your ego and admit that you are flawed, that you don't have the answer to every question, that it's okay to ask for help on things you're not 100 per cent certain about, and when you realise that you can let people in . . . that's the moment you can actually start moving forward.

Softening up is the hardest thing that some guys can imagine. In trying to be the hardest nut in the room, we often don't develop those emotional muscles which are really important. Which is a real shame, because that capacity for big feelings is what makes being alive so awesome. It's fundamental.

For me, that's one of the big ironies of the whole 'bloke' thing. Building strength and resilience actually requires developing your softer side and vulnerability. You can be the staunchest tough nut on any given day, but if you never let softness in, it gets that much harder to roll with the punches.

If you can never bend, then you can only break. And that capacity to bend and bounce back – what Tom Harkin likes to call 'range' – is something we need in life, because now and again, no matter how hard you are, life is going to find a way to tackle you right into the mud. That's part of the caper, like it or not. So, it's best to learn how to like it.

CHAPTER 2

BE YOURSELF, EVERYONE ELSE IS TAKEN

It was the end of the 2017 AFL season. What I should probably call, 'the worst day of my life'. At the time, it might have felt close. Looking back, it's the best thing that's ever happened to me.

You might think we'd have been wrapping up, but the last day at the club is as busy as the first. A lot of the day-to-day business of being an AFL player happens off-field – all the training, but also rehab, conditioning, psych – so there's a lot of catchups with different professionals the club employs. I looked at my schedule and had a day full of meetings – end-of-year medical, plans for training and conditioning, etc. I remember sitting in a room with our weights guy going through my orders for the next year, 'We want you to come back stronger,' and all of that talk.

But once I saw that my final meeting of the day was with Bolts, I knew it was all for show. And so did everyone else.

'Dylan, look,' Bolts said, soon as I walked in, nice and direct without sugar-coating it. 'There's no place for you on the list next year.'

And that was that. Band-Aid ripped off, nice and quick. I'd officially been sacked as a player for the Carlton Blues.

'That's okay,' I said and shook Bolts' hand.

I can't say I hadn't seen it coming. All through 2017, form and injury had meant I'd played only one game, and as the year had drawn to a close, the club hadn't approached me with next year's contract. But honestly, even those first couple of years at Carlton when I wasn't injured, I hadn't been working for it nearly hard enough. Instead, I'd sort of waited around just expecting things to happen. *In the twos*, I'd said to myself. *I'm 18 years old now, I'm young, I'm skinny, I'll develop, and next year they'll move me to the seniors*. But then I was 19, then 20, and quite quickly I started seeing the guys drafted below me move into the seniors while I stayed still.

Then they were lapping me. Because they were a lot hungrier. They'd had to push so much harder than I'd had to even to get to the start of race, so when they met me there waiting, their momentum left me in the dust. Honestly, the head start my dad's legacy had given me turned out to be more like a handicap – and not the good-for-your golfing kind. I would have been better off ripping up my birth certificate instead of thinking, *Lovely, my time is on its way*. You can't have that mindset. What I needed to say was, 'I'm ready

NOW!' And even if I wasn't, just worked towards it. If you keep sitting there waiting your dreams will never come. You'll find yourself waiting forever.

That's not something I really understood until I got this incredible feedback around the end of my second year at Carlton, from Heath Scotland. He was a real leader at the Blues back then and absolutely one of the toughest players to ever play the game. A dead-set legend, I absolutely loved the guy and admired him hugely as a footballer, too. He's everything I should have aspired to be. One day after training, Heath pulled me aside and gave me some uncomfortable truths.

'How long have you got left on your deal?' he asked.

'I'm out at the end of next year.'

'Dylan,' he said, 'you're not working hard enough. You're going to blink and your career will be over.'

Like me, Heath generally played midfield or half-back and he was getting on in years. He was just over 30 at this point, and theoretically, I should have been battling for his position.

'You should be champing at the bit to get my spot,' he told me, 'but I'm feeling absolutely no pressure from you. I don't feel threatened by you at all.'

Basically he told me that my work ethic was all wrong, that it was clear I didn't know what I was doing on the field, and that if I didn't improve I would be out on my arse. None of it was said out of disrespect, he was just telling me the things I really needed to hear. Because he *did* want to feel pressure from me and *did* want to see me take his spot on the team. Heath was one of the best teammates you could ever have; an incredible person with an amazing mind for what makes a team work.

He liked me as a guy, knew I was a quality person to have a beer with on the weekend, but had worked out, quite accurately, that I was at Carlton to have fun, not to win at all costs. The problem, as Heath saw it, and as he helped me see it too, was that I'd been trying to be everyone's mate instead of earning their respect.

Things started to change after that. Heath followed up that conversation and took me under his wing a bit. From there we went into serious training and he became a massive mentor for me in terms of showing me, one session at a time, how to work and improve as a team player. After that, I truly started to understand what it meant to belong on a team – how to go out on the field as part of one mighty unit instead of just Dylan Buckley tearing about the field on his own. That was when I played the best footy of my life. The season after Heath's quiet word to me I played 18 games in the seniors.

Problem was, as much as I pushed it at training and had finally learned my place in the team, my anxiety kept growing and growing. Anxiety had got its claws into me from a young age and it just kept getting worse. The more games I played, it seemed, the worse it got and at that stage in my life, I hadn't quite figured out how to label it or how to deal with it. So, despite my best intentions, my footy career kept sliding further and further backwards, until that inevitable, final meeting in Bolts' office.

I walked into Bolts' office as a Carlton AFL player and walked out as just me, Dylan Buckley. I'd played for the Carlton Football Club for nearly a decade, my entire adult life. Footy had been a childhood dream, and it had come true, and now it was time to wake up. I'd been delisted.

It's a very harsh word, delisting – it basically means you've been given the sack. It's just as crushing and as much of a financial stress, the only difference being that half of Australia gets to read about it in the paper. It's more polite to say that a player retires, maybe, but no – I was definitely delisted. It was a tough one. Objectively, delisting is one of the most savage things that can happen to a young footy player. The elephant in the room is that you couldn't cut it – that, for one reason or another, you failed. But I like to think that failures depend on how you look at them. Delisting was the lowest point, of probably the hardest year, of my life. But in other ways, it was the best.

I left the club on really good terms. The relationships I made there, the mates I made along the way, were and still are, unbelievable positives in my life. But I was physically done and mentally exhausted. In lots of ways I was glad to finish up. It was good to have closure. I walked out of Bolts' office with a lot of love and gratitude for the man and the team.

I gave the boys a hug and thanked them for everything they'd done for me. I meant it, too. I'd known this was on the way, which had given me a bit of time to come to grips with it – self-awareness is one of my best traits and probably one of my worst as well. If I'd been a bit more oblivious, I would have missed all the signs pointing to the fact that my career at Carlton was coming to an end. Instead, I left with good memories and one big question. *Well shit*, I thought to myself. *What do I do now?*

I looked to the future and didn't know what that would be. I knew I wanted to do my own thing and be my own man. The only issue was, I had no idea what 'being your own man' actually looked like. I'd lost my job, which I'd been expecting. What I hadn't factored in was losing my identity at the same time.

Mine wasn't the kind of profile that was going to kick down doors to opportunity. For the first time in my life I had no clear, obvious move forward. The life paths I'd planned on were shut. If I'd have played a couple of hundred more games, won a flag or two, then I could have been one of those guys who walks straight into a media gig, or a job with a corporate sponsor – the usual options laid out for post-footy life. Instead I had a mortgage in Melbourne, no job, no qualifications and few prospects.

I realised I didn't actually have anything anchoring me to the ground without footy. I look back now and see that it was a really exciting time, but in the moment, I was shit-scared. The thing that scared me most was the realisation that, without footy, I didn't really know who I was. I'd grown up with this core belief – I was a footy player. Without it, my ego took a pretty serious hit.

Ego – the good, the bad and the ugly

Probably my favourite thinker on ego, ambition and achievement is Chris 'Juddy' Judd. For those into AFL, Juddy needs no introduction, pretty much anyone who's been within cooee of the MCG knows who he is and what he has achieved. One of the best players of the modern game, he captained the West Coast Eagles, Carlton and the All-Australian teams. He's a three-times John Nicholls (Carlton's Best and Fairest), dual Brownlow and 2021 AFL Hall of Fame recipient . . . the list goes on.

As a kid, to watch him play was a masterclass. When I was growing up there were a lot of great players, but he was something else. On the midfield he was explosive – his speed, agility and strength saw him receive the ball in traffic, weave around the opposition and kick straight between the sticks. In one game Juddy would manage more tackles, disposals and goals than some players would in a season. In his later career, when injury slowed him down, he changed up his playing style, working smarter and harder to continue to bring home wins for the team. He showed almost superhuman ability in his skills on the field, as well as incredible wisdom, even as a young player. All of that took an unbelievable amount of work – his diet, training, recovery and psychological game are some of the most impressive the AFL has ever seen. And it got results. All of which is to say, he knows what he's talking about when it comes to achievement.

Juddy speaks about the idea of 'entitlement' – a word that has a bit of a negative connotation these days. Pick up any newspaper and you'll find an editorial moaning about how people – usually the younger generation – are 'too entitled these days'. It's meant as an insult, but when Juddy came on the pod we had a good chat about this, among many things.[3] He tells me that entitlement can be a positive attitude, provided you've done the work.

Entitlement can be a positive attitude, provided you've done the work.

'There are certainly people that feel they're entitled to something which they haven't earned. That's viewed as a negative, and so it should be,' says Juddy. 'But it's just as destructive when people don't think they're entitled to the good things that happen in their life.'

Entitlement in reverse

According to Juddy, feeling unentitled or unworthy of the rewards of your hard work will hold you back. It's too easy to fall into a negative mindset wherein you view setbacks and obstacles as a punishment for ambition rather than a natural part of life: *Well of course this would happen to me, because that's what happens . . . this is what always happens to me, poor me.* Too much thinking like this and pretty soon, in a competitive environment, you just stop fighting back.

You can also use entitlement in the reverse way – as a sort of anchor to help you bounce back when things don't go your way. If you believe that you deserve life's wins because you really have put the work in, and manage that thought along with a healthy level of entitlement, it becomes a powerful tool for motivation and resilience. A person with a healthy level of entitlement will think, when something bad happens to them, *Well, I guess that's just not how it's meant to work out for me. But I know I've done the work, so I'm going to adjust and adapt and live to fight another day.*

That dynamic happened in the AFL. There was such a difference between players who, regardless of raw talent, had a strong sense of entitlement and those who didn't. Those with a healthy attitude to what they deserved were able to pick themselves up from the losses more easily, rather than viewing them as evidence that they were doomed to fail. They'd listen to the feedback, come up with a plan, respond and come back bigger and better. That healthy sense of entitlement becomes a hugely powerful thing for people, says Juddy.

That idea really resonates with me. In those early years I definitely carried a bit of an unearned sense of entitlement. For most of my footy career I had this sense that I was meant to be in the AFL and that success was going to happen, without fully comprehending what I needed to do to *make* it happen. In a way, I think it was a form of self-sabotage – because I believed I was already across the finish line, I stopped sprinting.

Your only competition is yourself

For all of us there comes a pivot point where you have to take stock of what you need to do to earn the things you want – whether in your sporting, personal or business life. You want to feel that if you put in the work you're entitled to expect good things to come to you. But it's a fine balancing act.

What that reward is – the work it requires and how hard you're willing to work to get it – really comes down to you in the end. The goals you set for yourself, the markers of success, the entitlements you're prepared to work towards – though they may be hazy in the distance, in most circumstances, you can roughly measure how much pressure you're willing to take on.

Life is competitive, especially for young males, but ultimately, if you set your own markers of success, you're only in competition with yourself. As Juddy puts it: 'If you're trying to outrun a bear that's trying to eat you and your mate, you don't have to outrun the bear, you've just gotta outrun your mate.'

It's a great image. I find it helpful to imagine 'my mate' not as a separate person, but my alter ego and the unfair expectations I put on myself. Ultimately, I'm only racing up against my idea of who I am. It's up to me to learn how to outrun the negative version.

Where I was supposed to run towards, though, was the big question. In terms of my post-AFL career, I had no idea what that next step for me was supposed to be. I can't say I didn't try and figure it out, or that I didn't have help. The AFL is really good for young players on that front. It cops a lot of flak and there are youngsters who get chewed up by the lifestyle and can't adjust to a post-footy world – but you can't say the AFL doesn't provide opportunities. While you're contracted they encourage you to go out and study or pursue extra-curriculars to help when you eventually transition out of the game. They'll make room in your schedule to empower you and even pay for your university fees.

That said, they only pay for your schooling if you see it through. The amount of HECS debt I've paid because I didn't know you had to unenroll from a course you've dropped is ridiculous. I went to uni thinking I would do PE teaching. That lasted a couple of weeks each at Victoria Uni and then La Trobe. Then I did a Certificate IV in building and construction which I passed, but only by copying everyone else's work. I also tried real estate, did a carpentry course – I failed at just about everything. I was trying to work out what to do with my life, but gee-whiz, it wasn't cheap.

I wasn't the most studious person. At all. But I was trying new things to find some direction in life because, in all honesty, I was pretty lost. Mainly because I used to think that everyone had the world figured out and I was the only one who didn't. Much later, after years of talking to people – successful, happy, got-their-shit-together sort of people – I realised the most amazing truth of the world: *nobody* knows what they're doing, they're all just making it up as they go along. We all fail, but the smart ones fail hard and learn fast on the way. And there's another common theme among these successful folks too: their willingness to make mistakes – knowing that each one brings them a little closer to figuring out what the goal looks like for them.

Nobody knows what they're doing. They are just making it up as they go along. We all fail, but the smart ones fail hard and learn fast on the way.

Lord of the cringe

It always pays to be able to laugh at yourself. Take the serious stuff seriously, yeah, but it doesn't have to be life-and-death the whole time. I actually had one of my biggest epiphanies precisely because I was taking the piss out of myself. Like all my best stories, it started with me losing. Specifically, it started with me losing a drinking game.

I was at a party with a few other players and we were playing this drinking game. We agreed that the loser would have to hand their Instagram account over for the rest of the party to make a post that had to be kept up for 24 hours. The idea was to write the most embarrassing, cringe, extra, taking-the-piss-out-of-inspo-memes post.

Naturally, I lost. So they put up this photo of me with a super-earnest caption over the top: 'I'm going to be captain of Carlton, I'm the best . . .' string-of-nonsense inspirational wisdom, Facebook-memes-that-your-aunt-posts sort of stuff, which ended with a quote from – supposedly – old mate Oscar Wilde: 'Remember to be yourself, as everyone else is taken.'

I remember reading it, laughing and thinking, *That's funny, they've nailed me here.* I do have a tendency to hammer away with the deep and meaningfuls. And then I got to the end and thought, *that's a really fucking good quote: be yourself, everyone else is taken.*

I loved it. I thought, *I'm going to actually steal that and embrace it and use it.* So, I ended up adopting it as a kind of personal motto which, years later, would become the tagline for my podcast, *Dyl & Friends*. It became a sort of origin story for me. Because, as all good jokes reveal, I was actually pretty close to the image in that meme. I wasn't a typical lad, really. Nobody is when you get down to it. We pretend we are, but deep down, we've got a lot more going on.

I love my mates, but I'm not really about binge-drinking and punting and all of that. I do my own thing. I work in media and love hanging out with the missus and watching movies and crying at the sad bits. Why would I be embarrassed by that? It's just who I am. So, I embraced it and learned to be comfy in my own skin. I say that like it's an easy process, but of course, it's not. It's *hard as* for some people. But I'm going to tell you how I got there. Strap in. There's going to be some inspirational quotes.

Let's develop a tool kit

One thing which surprises a lot of people about modern AFL is how much mental health stuff is done on a regular basis. There are a lot of meetings focusing on the mindset of players and our psychological wellbeing. You get drafted on your physical skills, you've got some talent and some drive, but nothing can really prepare you for the mental challenge of being a player. It's crazy to think about. You're 18 years old and suddenly you're working in a professional organisation. You're on TV, reporters are asking for quotes – who you're dating, what you're wearing. It's weird. At the same time, you're trying to excel in the game at an elite level and deal with the pressure and stress that comes with it all. So, a lot of the training you get as a fresh AFL player must necessarily be about learning to manage all that, because it's a lot for a young guy to handle.

To be honest, when I was 18, I took that stuff about as seriously as any kid would. I was there to play footy, not to listen to a psychologist talk about managing anxiety and my emotional state. I hated it, absolutely hated it, wasn't interested in lectures on mental health at all. But that probably reflected where I was at as a player – my game slipping away, but not understanding why. I'm very lucky that I just got the message drilled into me so repetitively that it finally started to sink in. Because, as with most things mindset- and mental-health-related, it took practice. The thing that helped most in the end was training my brain to be responsive and open to learning new things.

As a player, you sit in those meetings and you're not really tuning in, but then something – a tool or technique for practising mindfulness, let's say – catches your ear and you're like, *Oh, wow, that's pretty cool.* You think about it for a while and then you forget about it. It gets tucked away in the back of your mind. Then a situation comes up and – good to go – you have this tool to help you deal with it.

It's almost like, the more you hear and start collecting different mental health management techniques, the more well equipped you become to deal with life's ups and downs. You take that technique and pop it into your tool belt, and then another, and then another, and suddenly you've got all those tools strapped on. So now you know you've got them and how to use them when you need to.

I should make something very clear at this point. Everything I'm talking about in this book is from my personal experience. I'm sharing what I know and discussing what I find works for me personally. What might be a life-saving tool for me might not necessarily be helpful for the next guy.

Some of this I learned at footy and other bits 'n' bobs through my podcast guests. I call these things 'tools' and that's exactly how I think of them. When I come across a tool I like, for example, a two-minute meditation to help with pre-game nerves, I tuck it away for when I need it. Just like a tradie keeps what he needs on his tool belt – a hammer, a wrench, whatever – and reaches back to grab it when he needs it, I do the same when managing my mental health and relationships. These tools can be mental (like thinking a certain way) or physical (like taking deep breaths to short circuit an adrenaline rush), but they are there on the toolbelt when I need them.

That said, just because a tool works for someone doesn't mean that it's going to work for everyone. You have try out different things and pick the ones that work best for you. Everyone is different. I've definitely fallen into the trap of trying many different things and hoping they'll work, but not sustaining them in the long term. Which is great – it's awesome to try new things and experiment with new techniques to find what fits you as an individual. Over time, you can look at the evidence of what's worked for you in the past and bring that into your everyday. So here ya go, your first set of tools.

Identity Toolkit

- Remember the golden rule: nobody knows what they are doing. It takes time to figure out who you are and what you're going to be, so don't sweat it.
- Entitlement is a two-edged sword. If you think you deserve something but never work for it, you'll never get it. But at the same time, knowing that you've earned something will power you through the hard times.
- It's okay to cry. In fact, it feels great. Go ahead and give it a try.
- Individuality is an amazing gift. Remember to be yourself – everyone else is taken.
- Self-esteem is important, but it also pays to be able to laugh at yourself. Take the serious stuff seriously, yeah, but it doesn't have to be life-and-death the whole time. Don't let your ego get in the way of enjoying yourself.
- In the long run, the only person you're in competition with is yourself. Like Juddy says, if you're running from a bear, you only need to run to outrun your mate aka your alter ego.

ANXIETY

CHAPTER 3

CAVING IN UNDER PRESSURE

I'm an anxious person, always have been.

But geez, I hate the word 'anxiety' – it feels like such a buzz word these days. In fact, I hate it so much, I didn't even want this chapter in the book. I actually asked if we could remove it, then realised I'd have to change the title of the book if we did, because it wouldn't be an honest chat.

Younger me didn't want to acknowledge that anxiety was something I was dealing with in my life. Internally, I'd rip into myself, *You're a pussy mate, why are you so weak? . . . Just do it, you're so embarrassing.* But honestly, anxiety has been with me for as long as I can remember.

My earliest memories are of being anxious. As a little kid, when Mum was driving me somewhere and stopped to put petrol in the car, I would freak out when she went in to pay. I don't know why, but when she would leave me and my sister in the car for the two minutes it would take to get to the counter and back, I would become convinced she was never coming back. My sister was fine, but I would have to go into the shop with Mum, or I was sure that she'd disappear somehow.

I just hated leaving Mum by herself. Even being dropped off at school would set me off. Going on school camps wasn't an option. Until I was in Year 10, I never slept away from home. I didn't stay over at friend's houses or go to slumber parties because of the massive anxiety it would give me. If I tried going, Mum would stay awake because she knew around midnight, she would get a call asking her to come and pick me up. That happened all through childhood, right up until I was 16 or so. At that point I had no choice because footy was taking me all over the country.

Ahh, AFL. Not exactly a relaxing job for someone prone to anxiety (though, at that point, I had no idea that's what I had or what to call it). When you're a top-level footy player, every single thing you do on the field is broadcast to the country and recorded for the rest of time. Every goal, mark, every time you touch the ball is recorded in the stats and goes into sporting history. You go into a game knowing that if you mess up, it'll probably be in the papers the next day and that while you're out there, someone in the stands is definitely going to let you know how they feel about it. The level of scrutiny and judgement on the player is extraordinary. If they measured anxiety levels, I'm sure I would have walked away with a medal for that, eight years running.

In retrospect, anxiety was probably the biggest negative factor on my footy career by far. I didn't see it until my career finished, but my anxiety was pretty bad. Since I've been learning about mental health and consciously working to understand that part of myself, I've realised that my anxiety took all the joy out of footy for me once I started playing in the seniors. I just loved footy to bits, but I couldn't enjoy it the way I had before I'd gone into the AFL.

Game days were the worst. In the lead up to every game I would hope that it'd be called off, or that I'd wake up and the coach would go, 'You know what, Dyl? You don't have to play today. We're going to hold you over in case of emergency.'

Anxiety made it impossible to function at peak performance. For me, anxiety was just as debilitating as a physical injury. Worse, really. I thought the times I was injured were the lowest points of my career, but in hindsight, they were when I felt happiest as a team player because the pressure was off. If something in my body snapped or broke or tore I'd be flooded with relief as I limped off-field because I'd know that I had four weeks off from having to face game day again.

There were times I could get out of my head and the anxiety left me alone. That was where I played my best footy. I once kicked a bit of a miracle goal against the Bulldogs, probably because I didn't have time to think about it. I was playing defence, way back on the field, not really in a position to be scoring goals. Some of the spectators probably thought I was having a pie in the stands I was that far back. But then the ball came bounding up. I saw it, grabbed it, gave a little spurt of speed up the boundary and banged the ball up. I don't know how it worked logistically, but it sailed straight through the goalposts and into history. Definitely one of the good ones.

A Bulldogs fan leaned over the fence. I thought I was about to cop a spray, but he instead he thumped me on the back and yelled, 'Onya!' It was really weird. My teammates reckoned it was a sympathy clap because I so rarely got a kick.

Most of the time, though, I was too anxious to react like that. Look, I know everyone gets anxious at times, it's very prevalent in footballers, but mine was out of control. I remember stretching during warm-ups before a game, really going for it and hoping I would tear my hammy off the bone because then I wouldn't have to go out there. But then I'd go out and something would click and I'd play some of the best footy of my life. Even though I was under the MCG lights surrounded by the roaring crowd, all of that slipped into the moment and I really became part of the game.

But then I'd go into the rooms at half-time and the anxiety would crush me again. *Alright, how can I get out of the next half? I don't fucking want to be here.* I could be playing incredibly well, kicking goals, but every break the panic kicked in and I'd start thinking about ways to get out of the game. The second I had a moment to worry, the anxiety just poleaxed me.

Which is pretty tragic, because I loved footy. The game itself is a lifelong passion and I love everything about it. I loved being part of the team. It was like hanging out with 40 of your best mates every day, getting paid to stay fit, go to the beach and play a game you love. Literally, my *work* was playing a *game*. I was so fucking lucky and I loved every minute of it. Except for game day, when my mental state took all the joy out of it. Since then I've learned what anxiety is and how it was affecting me, but at the time I didn't think my headspace was anything out of the ordinary. I'd just always felt that way, so I thought it was normal to feel so terrible.

Early in life, I was always nervous. I thought I was just scared or a 'pussy'. I was embarrassed about how weak it made me playing footy and didn't want to talk to anyone about it . . . 'What do you mean you don't want to be out on the field?' I thought they would say. I wanted to enjoy footy and I wanted to excel. At the time I would beat myself up for not competing with the other players, even though we trained the same amount. And truth is, I trained as hard as I could – I didn't fail for lack of effort or passion. My anxiety was so bad that it kicked my legs out from under me. I tried my guts out, but anxiety got in the way of me performing at my best.

It was bad even when I wasn't playing on the big stage. I remember the last professional game I ever played. It was for the Giants, in the twos, out in the suburbs of Brisbane against local team, the Aspley Hornets. Realistically, it was the lowest-stakes game of professional footy possible in Australia. Ninety percent of fans wouldn't even know it was happening – it wasn't televised, there was nobody in the stands. I knew that this was my last game, that no one was watching, and in the big picture, the outcome of the game didn't mean anything to either me personally or the team. And still, I felt like the anxiety would kill me.

I couldn't even eat breakfast before the game. The whole way there I was hoping the bus would break down, or crash, or something would happen to erase the game from Earth before I had to lace up my boots. Just a stream of pure fucking anxiety attacks coming out of nowhere. *This is so random? Why is this happening now?* I asked myself. I didn't understand it. It's something I'm still working on understanding. Because I loved footy. Everything about it. Except for the anxiety that swallowed me whenever I wasn't burning up in the joy of the game in the moment.

It's not something that got better over my career either, but worse as my footy was wrapping up and I saw delisting on the horizon. When footy finished I thought it would go away, but it didn't. Later it showed up in other areas of my life, like podcasting – freaking out after releasing an episode, worried that something might be taken the wrong way.

Eventually I started getting help from professionals on how to manage it, and started educating myself on anxiety and how it affects me. 'Name it to tame it' has worked for me – understanding what I have, its symptoms and how they affect me, helps me manage my anxiety better these days, although it's still a work in progress.

One of my biggest keys is getting my foundations right – the four pillars: health, fitness, diet and sleep. I check in with myself regularly on these to help keep my life as balanced as possible. These four pillars underpin everything else in my life and keeping on top of them allows me to be the best person I can be – for myself and everyone I care about. If I can get these four things right all the time, does it stop me feeling anxious? No, no guarantees, but it gives me the absolute best shot.

Sometimes I think about the career I could've had if I'd had the techniques to help me better manage that anxiety, but I don't have any real regrets. Because, while who knows how far I might have gone with footy, I've used it – the good and the bad – as motivation for the next phase. I may have missed the full opportunity because of my mental health, but I'm working to manage my anxiety to make sure I embrace my days ahead to the fullest possible extent. I've wasted enough time worrying about it.

To be honest, I still haven't worked out how to fix it. It's just one of those things I haven't nailed, and maybe it's okay if I never do. I'm trying to work towards a resolution, while knowing full well it's probably not something that can or needs to be totally 'fixed'. Anxiety sucks, but it's also what makes me who I am. It's my enemy and my best friend, because it makes me work how I do.

I'm a worrier – I take after my mum that way. Probably my dad too. But they were from a generation where mental health and self-care wasn't really part of the everyday conversation. So I'm lucky to have come up in an environment where awareness of anxiety and some better coping mechanisms are something I can access, that's for sure.

Many of those I learned through AFL, as you know, and some I continue to pick up through guests on my podcast and in various other ways, as you're going to read about. There are few things I can say that I know are absolutely true, but here's one of them: you never regret a swim. No matter how cold the water is, no matter how much you don't want to jump in, you never get out of the water regretting the experience. I've found a similar thing in going to therapy.

If you ever hit the gym to feel good, then give therapy a crack

I'd seen a therapist a few times when I was playing footy. At AFL clubs there's always a psychologist available for players who want to talk and we're encouraged to go see them. So, I had some experience of therapy, but it wasn't something I did regularly . . . Until the time came for the world's most difficult chat – when Dad and I had to deal with some confronting realities.

That was the first time I'd sought help under my own steam outside of a sports scenario. I knew things were going to get pretty tough, and as I headed into the situation I could feel the anxiety starting to build, so I went and found a psychologist. That's a process in itself – you see a GP, fill out and discuss a questionnaire so they can create a mental health care plan for you, and from that you'll likely get a referral to a psych which, if your condition qualifies, may initially be covered by Medicare – a little bit of work, but gee-whiz, the rewards are fucking huge.

My psych is great, very wise, smart as hell. She has a real talent for calling me out on certain ways of thinking and looking at life. She's helped me understand that a lot of the ways I tended to think about myself weren't just unhelpful, but straight-up wrong. It's amazing how someone with that skillset can equip you to see life more clearly.

Through that period of crisis with my dad she gave me some awesome tools to manage my anxiety and I still see her every few weeks now, just for a tune-up. Sometimes I go weekly, sometimes I go monthly, sometimes I don't go for months – there's no rules.

I find therapy just as helpful as eating well and getting my exercise. It's a mental release. Some people get that from religion, maybe, or from meditation. Or from golf – let's face it, I probably get some of it from golf – but therapy is definitely part of it. Even if it's not always easy. It's a lot like going for a run or going to the gym. Before you go, you're so sure you don't really want to, but as soon as you finish, you're like *Fuck, that was a good session. I could go again.* You never regret it after you've done the work and the work never really ends, but for me, therapy makes life steadily easier.

This all would have been a useful way to describe it to me when I was a young knucklehead. Because Australians – guys especially – attach a stigma to seeing a psychologist. And that's not good, because according to government statistics, one in every five Australian adults struggles with some kind of mental health problem every year.[4]

Even if you're not struggling in the moment, it never hurts to go in for a tune-up. Mental health is not the same thing as mental illness. It's about taking care of yourself. About training your mind, like we do our bodies – not just when you're struggling to survive, but before then: to thrive. I see mental health training as being proactive about getting the best from yourself. If you want to be an elite athlete, you hire a coach. So why wouldn't you hire a psychologist, too? Do you know who sees a psychologist? Tiger Woods. Serena Williams. Roger Federer. Nick Riewoldt. All pretty fucking good at what they do. Because they look after their bodies and their minds. Elite athletes at that level know better than anyone that strength and resilience are just as much a result of investing in your mental health as sweating it out in the gym.

Cold, discomfort and resilience

One of the best thinkers on resilience and stress management is David 'Butters' Buttifant. Butters is a former AFL player turned high-performance coach who's all about pushing yourself to learn how far you can go. When I was at Carlton he took the team to Arizona for a high-altitude training performance camp, where he put us through some of the toughest physical challenges imaginable.

One was climbing Mt Humphreys Peak, the tallest mountain in Arizona, way above the snowline. I'd never even seen snow before and barrelled straight into this Everest-basecamp-level altitude. That was tough. Even tougher – probably one of the most challenging things I've ever done physically and mentally – we walked down the Grand Canyon. It wasn't that hard to begin with, the first few hours were super easy, just strolling along like, *Cool, I'm in the Grand Canyon, what an amazing place.*

But after walking for two hours straight, I wasn't even halfway down. When I finally hit the bottom, absolutely knackered, I had to turn around and walk straight back up. I remember standing at the bottom of the canyon, looking up at the finish line all the way up in the sky, terrified of how much it was going to hurt. It's a slow incline, all the way down. I knew climbing up would be twice the effort of going down, the grind just slowly breaking you. Somehow, Butters got us through it.

Years later, in March 2021, Butters came on the podcast as a guest.[5] In the course of things, he invited me to come on the 'Resilience Builders' training camp he ran on Cradle Mountain in Tasmania. By then I'd finished with footy and was starting to realise I was getting *too* comfortable. That was something I wanted to change, because I've found that if I don't feel like I'm actively moving forward in life, then I'm probably going backwards. I felt ready to challenge myself, physically and mentally. That's something I really miss about footy, actually, constantly being challenged and being made to do things I don't really want to do and feeling amazing afterward for having done them. Spending hours in the gym, 2 km time trials, climbing mountains – all that stuff is heaps easier to do when it's literally your job. It's harder to keep pushing yourself to stay motivated when it's all up to you.

Training camp would be cold, hard and uncomfortable, Butters said, but if I wanted a challenge to shake me up, then this was it. So I said I'd go – and immediately regretted it. Luckily, right around then, Covid hit. Part of me was grateful. *Thank fuck, now I don't have to do all that.*

But eventually the Covid lockdowns passed and after that I had no excuses. I got on the inescapable flight to Tassie, absolutely dreading it – several aspects of the trip were really revving up my levels of anxiety. One was going into the wilderness with 10 other guys I didn't know. Another was being out of mobile phone range the whole time. That was a pretty serious barrier for me because I freak out if I don't have my phone. If I miss a call from my wife or mum, my mind immediately goes to the worst possibilities. *Oh shit, what's happened, who's died?* If I can't get onto someone, I'm immediately worried that something has happened to them. So I was freaking out about that, too.

But the thing I was dreading the most was the caving expedition into Mole's Creek caves. Planned for the end of our tour, it was supposed to be the highlight of the trip. For me, the prospect was an utter nightmare. I am extremely claustrophobic. Like, the thought of being holed up in the dark sends me literally batshit crazy. Maybe that's a bad analogy because bats probably like being in caves quite a bit. Me? Not so much. I hate being in a tight space with every cell in my body. *Hate* it. I *hate* being constricted. Have done my whole life.

One of my earliest memories is of playing with my sister when we were kids. She wrapped me up in a doona so tight I couldn't move. I completely lost it, absolutely freaked out. I just could not handle that feeling of being enclosed. Same with being in lifts – if there's a few people in there and it gets a bit hot and sweaty, I start to freak out.

I copped it badly at footy because I was good at getting myself injured, so I had to get scanned in the MRI machine all the time. When you're getting your shoulders or back scanned it takes a good 15 minutes for them to get the image – I'd be sweating every second. They'd slide me into the machine like a body on a slab and this huge donut-shaped machine would start spinning around me. Every nerve in my body would start screaming to get the heck out of there. It got to the stage where I had to be fully medicated, basically put to sleep, in order to get into the machine.

So, going into a cave wasn't very high on my bucket list – a fairly daunting test of my stress levels. Not something I wanted to do *at all.* I spoke to Butters before the trip because I wanted to give him the heads up that I didn't think I'd actually be able to make myself go underground. He assured me that was okay. 'No worries, man, you don't have to do anything you don't want to.'

We both knew that wasn't true. The whole point of the camp was to be forced out of my comfort zone. *She'll be right*, I thought, *I have the whole trip to get used to the idea. Plenty of time to psych myself up for it.* But, no. The second we landed in Tassie and found ourselves out in the wilderness, Butters turned around. 'Alright, we're going caving now. Everyone gear up. We're heading underground.'

I've probably never been so scared as I was in that prep session. I remember we were getting briefed as we started putting on the gear, going through all the instructions and safety and what to do in an emergency and I was freaking the fuck out. Anxiety through the roof which for me means: the sweats, the shakes and nausea. My heart starts going a mile a minute and my breathing gets weird. And then there's the emotional stuff.

Let's talk about panic attacks, real quick.

When they're really bad, you honestly believe you're going to die. Physically it feels like they say a heart attack is supposed to, with a big side order of intense dread. Imagine watching a horror movie while a little guy tries to punch his way out of your chest from the inside. A proper anxiety attack, if you don't know what you're experiencing, is truly terrifying. Even once you know what it is and know what you're going through, the anxiety will still trip you up and make the panic worse. Your body and mind have a sort of back and forth:

Body: 'I'm pretty sure this is it, Dyl. You're dying.'

Mind: 'I don't think so mate. This is just a bit of anxiety.'

Body: 'Are you sure mate? It seems pretty bad . . .'

Mind: 'It'll pass. Take some deep breaths. That'll help.'

Body: 'You're not breathing so well, buddy. Are you *sure* you're not dying? What if I squeeze these lungs a little more? Does that help?'

And so on.

So there I was going through a full bore five-star anxiety episode while kitting up. Luckily, Butters clocked the situation. He pulled me aside and had a bit of a talk with me to calm me down. He gave me a toolkit of three mental techniques that he wanted to share. 'When you start to feel that intense flush of anxiety,' he said, 'try these three things:

'*Go to your breath*.' Concentrate on your breath and work to steady it. In and out. Your breath powers the engine that keeps you alive. As long as you can draw breath, you'll be okay. Whatever's going on, just concentrate on breathing through it.

'*Go to your happy place*.' For example, mine is Bronte Beach. When I lived in Sydney, it was my favourite place and I have so many happy memories there. So I picture myself on the beach sitting on that grass just watching the waves and trying to calm down.

'*When all else fails, just fucking get it done*.'

I sat listening, waiting for more detail, but Butters was done.

'Oh, right,' I said, a bit surprised at how raw and rough option three was. 'I'll take that on board.'

I was used to anxiety management advice coming from psychs and specialists brought in by the AFL. All the advice I'd ever been given on talking myself around my anxiety had seemed polished and vague. I couldn't remember anyone ever being so direct.

When all else fails, just fucking get it done.

And look, nowadays there's probably an equal argument that persevering through panic could be detrimental. As I've said time and again, any tips I share in this book are purely what worked for me. If following Butters' advice is something you want to give a crack, then maybe try it first by pushing through a training run or swim as a better option . . . But as for me, I had a cave to conquer.

With Butters' strategies ringing in my ears, we went into the cave. It was dark and cold and the walls felt like they were closing in on me. In that moment, there was absolutely nothing I wanted to do less than put one foot in front of the other and go further into the dark. I was really starting to freak out. Time to launch into Butters' methods.

First I went to my breath, tried to meditate my way out of the panic. Nup. No good. Not working. Next I mentally took myself to Bronte – pictured waves crashing on the beach, blue water stretching forever, seagulls overhead . . . Nope. No crashing waves here, only my blood swooshing in my ears and my lungs struggling to get enough air. By now it was getting harder to breathe. My pack, my helmet, the rest of the safety gear felt like it weighed a ton. It hadn't felt that way putting it on, but now I felt crushed. I would have given *anything* to get out of there. But I knew I couldn't.

Even in the grip of the panic, I knew there was no way to escape. There was only one option left: just *fucking get it done.* I stepped into the cave, my body screaming at me that it would end me, like I may as well have been stepping into a bear-trap, my adrenaline was spiking so bad. But then my foot hit the cave floor and I exhaled for what must have been the first time in ages. One step down and I wasn't dead yet. I took another. Then a little further. Then after that, I was good.

I ended up having a great time in the cave, and ever since, I've had that third option in my toolkit. Now, when all my usual anxiety management techniques and tools just aren't working and I can't relax, I remember walking into that cave. It taught me that it's possible to make incredible things happen when you *just fucking do it.*

I'm not saying that option three is for every person or scenario, but I think Butters knew it would work for me. The way I'm built, sometimes I get so anxious about something that it's the only way to move forward. Knowing that is Butters' job – as a high-performance manager, it's his job to identify what makes people tick. Option three was a coping mechanism I could take on board for when I needed it. And when I did, I came out the other side with a new experience that proved my resilience.

'When you overcome a challenge or adversity, it becomes a wonderful reference point,' explains Butters. When he got me to experience and work through that very real discomfort and fear, handling the physiological stress from my emotional state wasn't easy. But I did it. It wasn't fun, but I proved to myself it was possible in that situation. Now, next time I find myself in an anxiety-inducing squeeze, I know what I'm capable of.

'That's how we can raise the bar and build our capacity,' says Butters. You build a tolerance to stress, learning to handle it more efficiently. Once you know it's possible to break past a threshold you'll be more efficient at doing it next time.

Remember your toolkit

Resilience building doesn't need to be as extreme as the example above. If you're stuck in *any* cave, whether metaphorical or literal, whatever gets you through the moment is probably what's going to work for you going forward. That's how you start to put your toolkit together. If Butters' three rules work for you, go ahead and put them on your toolbelt. And if they all sound like rubbish to you, fine too. In the end, your kit may end up very different to mine – yours is what works for you, mine is what works for me.

I've found that one of the best things for me is a bit of sweat. Being active – running, swimming, getting out in nature or even doing a bit of gardening. If I stop getting outside or working out, I start to notice the effect on my mental health. Another big benefit for me is just talking it out. Usually that's with Juzz because she knows me better than anyone. Hearing myself out loud talking to her, especially when I'm getting worked up about something, usually helps me realise how silly the situation is.

Those are simple things that help me keep on top of my anxiety, things I do every day to help myself along. But I also have Butters' option three in the back pocket in a crisis. If push comes to shove, I know I can power through. Even if it's something that scares the absolute shit out of me. Which is good, because my anxiety isn't going anywhere. It's part of me.

And like any relationship, it might be growing on me. In some respects, I really hate my anxiety. But on the other hand, I love it because it makes me who I am. While it can be quite debilitating at times, there are definite positives to the way anxiety manifests in me. I'm a worrier, which means that going into a situation, I'm going to think the worst . . . I analyse every single thing that could possibly go wrong. Then I look at every single angle to figure out how to solve everything that could possibly go wrong – finding answers for every possible outcome. I overanalyse until my brain feels like it's going to burst, and then . . . I throw caution to the wind and just barrel straight in, all guns blazing.

It's exhausting, sure, but it also means that when something *does* go wrong, I'm ready to respond and succeed. But like they say about boxing: everyone goes in with a plan, until you get punched in the face. So sometimes my anxiety has worked out well for me and sometimes it hasn't. Even if at times it's held me back and is really hard to deal with, it's also landed me in better places. To make the best of the situation you find yourself in, work with the mind and body you have on the day.

CHAPTER 4
NERVES: THE PRICE OF ADMISSION

Performance anxiety is something I struggled with my whole AFL career. For eight years, no matter how hard I worked, I never knew if my nerves were going to do me in on game day. My life might have been very different if I'd had a better understanding of the difference between nerves and full-blown performance anxiety. The idea that nerves are a positive, that they are the price of admission to something you really, truly care about, is still something I'm working on getting my head around.

Even though I know my way around a podcast by now, I still get nervous. All the time. On a weekly basis, I'm sitting down and talking with people who are giants in their fields. Genius-level thinkers, or comedians, or God-tier athletes, people I've grown up admiring. You never know which way a conversation is going to go. There are a million variables. But at the end of the day, I hit record on the mic and try and have the best chat I can.

If you can tweak your mindset so that those nerves become fuel instead of something that holds you back, that's fantastic. That's part of the caper – you have to be able to deal with it and find what works best for you. It's an idea I keep coming back to because it's forced me to deal with the fact I'll always have anxiety and it's up to me to look after myself. It's as much a part of me as my muscles and bones and all the rest of it. Like my back – it played up badly during footy and still gives me grief, but I've only got one, so I have to look after it. I can't live without a spine, and much as I would like to, I can't live without anxiety. So even when it's playing up I have to learn to live with it, flourish if I can.

I can't live without anxiety. So even when it's playing up I have to learn to live with it, flourish if I can.

In those times when I've been able to get through the immediate flush of anxiety and used it to work out all the angles with my over-analysing brain, a kind of magic happens. You've got the plan in place, but then, even if life throws you something unexpected, you can still adapt. You learn to go with the flow, be like a leaf in the wind. I could compare it to my best days of footy, those days I was out on the midfield – every guy on the team in his place, we've been coached, trained, drilled, there's all these layers of strategy in place – and something goes wrong. One of the best players on your side goes off with an injury, or the wind does something weird. Whatever it is you're ready for it, because you've thought ahead and prepared for the worst-case scenario.

One of the hardest things I struggled with as a young athlete was trying to perform when I was feeling shithouse. There were heaps of occasions when I was like, *I don't feel good today, I don't think I can play.* Even though I knew I had the skills and just had to do what I'd done so many times before, I just couldn't. At training, when it was just me and my mates running around in the sunshine, I could get the ball up the field and through the goals with my eyes closed, pretty much. But when it came to game day and the anxiety ramped up, my nerves just shattered.

One particular day, pre-game during the warm-up, I wasn't feeling good. My anxiety was peaking so bad I felt like I was on the edge of a proper panic attack. All I could think about was getting out of the game. I was wracking my brain trying to find a way out, like maybe I could say I'd done my hamstring in the warm-up and then they wouldn't make me go out onto the field. Literally, I was on the verge of faking an injury because I had the yips so bad. But somehow, I got out on the field and actually played one of the best games of my life. It was great to have that win, but the lesson I took from that was even more valuable: I'd shown myself that I didn't have to feel good to go out there and perform. I had no idea the science behind how that worked until I spoke to an expert who helped me understand why my anxiety tended to get worse the more I fought it.

Pain points: find 'em, then you can fix 'em

Jonah Oliver is a performance psychologist, one of the most respected and sought after in Australia. His expertise is in helping people, including some of the world's best athletes, function at their peak performance. Part of his practice is taking a complex psychological theory and simplifying it so his clients can digest and implement it. I was lucky enough to get him on the pod to share some of his insights.[6]

'I keep it clichéd and simple. I help people focus on the right thing at the right time,' is how Jonah describes his work. 'It's not really about making people more talented. My job is often just to help them get out of their own way and let their talent shine.'

Jonah coaches people to repeat winning behaviours more predictably, to build up a pattern of behaviour that leads to better performance. In that way, he says, your skills will remain available to you, even if your confidence takes a hit – which it will, because that's normal and we're human. We are emotional creatures. We have up days and down days. But just because our emotions vary, doesn't mean our competence should.

We are emotional creatures. We have up days and down days. But just because our emotions vary, doesn't mean our competence should.

'No matter who I am, there'll be days where I feel great, days where I feel crap, and days where I feel in-between. There'll be days where I feel doubtful, worried, anxious, angry – the usual tapestry of being a human.'

I couldn't relate to that any harder. When I told Jonah about my own struggles with panic and anxiety, he explained some of the neuroscience that was tripping me up.

Correlation versus causation

The human brain craves reason – wants to know *why* things happen to us. Humans evolved by learning to associate 'things' (or events) with 'outcomes'. So we tend to label the first event as the 'cause' and the second as the 'outcome', when usually, it's just a correlation between the two.

As Jonah explains it, we notice a relationship between events. Event A happened and then Event B happened. So, we assume Event A caused Event B. But that's not the case. There is a *correlation*, that is, they have some things in common (time or location, for example) which makes them seem linked somehow, but in actual fact, they are two completely separate events. One does not *cause* the other.

Picture a caveman, your grandad's grandad of many generations ago. He's sitting under a tree, drinking water from a stream and eating a red berry. Not long afterwards he gets crook. Now, he knows that *something* made him sick, but doesn't know if it was the red berry, the water, or the tree, so he associates all three with feeling crook and steers clear of them all in the future. No red berries, no water from that stream, no going near that tree. It's safer and it keeps him alive long enough to pass his genes on to the next generation.

It's the same mechanism that your brain uses today. From an evolutionary point of view, the human brain is very protective and prone to anxiety, because anxiety has kept our species alive since the Stone Age. Because of that, our brains look for correlations between events and things . . . and that's where superstitions come from. Lots of AFL players perform lucky superstitions before they go out for a game, you probably have some yourself. You might eat Weet-Bix for breakfast before a big exam or presentation, or maybe you have a lucky pair of jocks you wore once on a good day and now you wear them every time you need to feel powerful. That's the correlation part of your brain at work – the magic of neuroscience, not actual magical jocks.

So all those times I went out onto the field with my confidence zapped by anxiety I was shooting myself in the foot because I'd convinced myself my nerves wouldn't let me play my A game. Which then made me frustrated because I wasn't playing to my potential. Later on, that frustration would cool to disappointment and distress.

'I call it the athlete's triad,' Jonah says. 'Anxiety before an event, anger and frustration during it, then sadness afterwards.'

The good news is that it's not something you have to fight against to perform at your best. Jonah's approach is to flip the relationship between nerves and anxiety and move to what's called 'an acceptance-based model'.

Nerves are the price of entry

'We worry about things we care about. So, naturally, anytime we're doing something that matters, we'll be nervous prior to it,' Jonah says. 'If you wanna do hard things, there's a price of entry and that might mean you feel some anxiety, some nerves, some pre-game uncertainty.'

Put another way, because of our caveman-correlative brains, we learn to link our nerves with the outcome of poor performance.

'For example, I felt nervous and I didn't play well. Then when nerves show up again I think, *Oh, that's gonna mean I'm not gonna play well again*. But that's correlation, there's no causation,' says Jonah.

In that situation, we start to think we need to get rid of the nerves in order to perform.

'So, we're sitting there pre-game, getting nervous, going, *Oh, I can't feel this way*. We then try to get rid of our nerves and usually fail, which then sets us on fire emotionally. So then all our focus turns to how we're feeling.'

From a psychological point of view that helps me understand why my anxiety held me back on the footy field. Not because I was nervous, but because I was in this loop of *worrying about* my nerves. My focus was on my anxiety and trying to get rid of it instead of on trying to get the ball up the field. My head wasn't in the game because it was worried about the fact that I was worried.

'If we can free ourselves up from that and realise that we can still play normally, competently, and do our thing whilst feeling the anxiety, then we're freed up and we've broken that correlational relationship,' says Jonah.

The way to do that is to look differently at setbacks; learn to make room for that discomfort. Jonah says that perfectionism, obsession – those traits you see a lot in athletes – have positive sides to them. It means you're driven, you're motivated, you work hard and you have high standards. But those traits can also be debilitating when you get too caught up in the fear of failure and can't accept the possibility of a bad outcome.

'So, acceptance – what does that mean?' Jonah asks. 'It means learning that tough, internal experiences are normal, they're okay and don't have any impact on my performance if I can just let them be there.'

It's about growing your capacity to sit with more discomfort, not fight to get rid of it.

'Hey, how about we just let the brain be a brain?' Jonah suggests to his clients. 'Because what's more important? *Feeling* good or *playing* good? Trying to get rid of your nerves, or just letting them be there and instead focusing on doing the right thing at the right time and going after what's important to you?'

At the top-line, Jonah's approach helps athletes bring their focus in line with their skills. That means, they can repeat what they know they are capable of in training when it really matters: on the sports field, in competition where there's intense pressure. Part of how he does that is by helping athletes work out exactly what's holding them back, mentally.

Jonah uses his knowledge of psychology to identify the 'pain points' in an athlete's performance. If, for example, he's working with a golfer who gets nervous at the critical point of a tournament, he finds ways for them to practise playing through the nerves and improve their wedge game, or putt, or whatever it is they need to make the shot.

'If I can help my golfers save one shot at the pointy end of the thing, that could mean the difference between being 50th in the world or top 10th in the world,' Jonah says. 'And that's the biggest lever we can use to help improve performance.'

Often, athletes will come to him because they have identified a deficit in their game, but don't know how to fix it. He uses the analogy of going to the dentist with a toothache.

'I'll go to the dentist and say, "My tooth hurts. I know that. I don't know what's required to stop it hurting though, just please fix it." That's the dentist's job. So, that's sort of the approach I take.'

Athletes can normally identify many of their pain points. They know what's wrong, but they don't have the expertise to know what might help. By the time they begin working with Jonah they've probably tried a whole bunch of things to try to fix their issues, but are still not getting the outcome they want. It's Jonah's job to work with them and try different options to remove those pain points and reach those goals.

Confidence versus competence

One of the most common things Jonah gets asked for help with is confidence. Individual athletes worry that they are struggling with low confidence, or a coach wants their team to be more confident.

'There is this obsession with confidence because the belief is, "If I feel confident, I'll play well." Whereas what they're really saying is they want *competence*.'

Jonah defines the difference between the two. Confidence is an emotion: you feel a certain way. Competence is a behaviour: you can do something well. Say I'm playing footy and I feel like I'm absolutely dominating – that's confidence. But the skills I'm actually using to get the ball and kick it through the sticks? That's competence.

'Me at a karaoke bar with six beers in my belly? I'll jump up on that stage and belt my lungs out, but I can't sing. It doesn't matter how confident I am, I can't sing. There's plenty of people out there who have amazing voices, but they're too caught up in their story to get up on stage and have a go.'

Basically, as anyone who's been in that situation can agree, confidence doesn't actually mean you're any good at singing in key or hitting those high notes.

'So, in life and in sport, we've got to focus more on bringing people's *competencies* out, not searching for this idea that we have to be *confiden*t before that can happen. Confidence actually follows competence.'

Jonah points out that even athletes and coaches get the concepts mixed up. When a team plays a good game and the captain talks about being super confident out on the field, they're subconsciously connecting confidence to competence. Which is not really helpful or accurate, because the emotion of confidence isn't actually the deciding factor to how a physical game plays out. The ball doesn't know what you're thinking and feeling. When you kick the ball between the sticks it's because you have behaved competently, not because you impressed it with your confidence.

'We think that the reason we played well was because we felt confident [where really] we displayed competent behaviours,' explains Jonah. In his view, the conflation of confidence and competence is counterproductive, because it gives us the idea that you can only be good at what you do when you're feeling confident and good in your abilities. A better mindset is to lean into your skills and muscle memory, rather than your emotional state. 'If I can just connect to my competence and let go of my attachment to needing to feel confident, then I'm now much more likely to be consistent.'

Competition is an ordinary performance on a special day

As a coach of Olympians, Jonah says they have one trait in common. 'They're really, really boring,' he says with a laugh. 'That's my playfulness, but I encourage them to go to the Olympics and be really boring.

'When they go to compete, of course, they're fully aware of how big the occasion is. Of course, it matters! It's the bloody Olympics! Their once-in-a-lifetime event. So, there's an extra magnitude of "the fear of failure" and all its trimmings.' In training for this, Jonah has them develop a mindset to go out there and be as normal as possible, to replicate the best results from their training.

'This idea that you have to be in a really fixed psychological state in order to perform well is absolute garbage. You have to be in a state of focus and connected to the behavioural outputs that you're required to do which allow that typically to happen.

'Competition is an ordinary performance on a special day,' Jonah tells me. So, it's important 'not to try to deny the specialness of it.'

You can't lie to your brain. Your brain knows when something means the world to you. I know for myself, before a game I was really excited and nervous and worried and hopeful and doubtful. And anxious. But while I lived trying to fight that anxiety for eight years, Jonah helps his athletes to get ready for the nervousness, butterflies and feels that come with the specialness of the day.

'So, you go out there and really connect to the replication of your skill. And that's your safety blanket,' he explains. 'You don't then need to fight your nerves or fight your brain or control what's going on internally. You just anchor to your performance.'

Jonah says that's one of the key measures of a champion performance in any field. Olympic athletes, racing car drivers, UFC fighters, surgeons, business leaders, it doesn't matter.

'It's understanding that the job is to train at a level that the sport demands, or even beyond. So then you can show up when it really matters.'

One of Jonah's clients is Cameron Smith, the God-level golfer who I watched play in the British Open in 2022. Absolutely astonishing golf on show that day from Cam. He was on the 17th hole, traditionally one of the hardest holes in the course, and hit his ball into a terrible spot. An absolutely horrible spot – there was a massive bunker literally opposite him. I would have lost my freaking mind in that position. But Cam was so calm. He just walked up to the ball, looked at it almost like he was bored, and then punted it up over this hill, walked up, did it again and made one of the most magnificent clutch putts I've ever seen.

Jonah was there coaching Cam that day and says he was anything but calm in those final five holes. While Cam did his usual grounding mindfulness and resetting, he reached for his water bottle, 'and nearly choked to death on international TV because his throat wouldn't swallow. That's how nervous he was.'

Because, as Jonah reminded me, Cam is human. He knew the score, knew he was playing a major. It mattered to him. The roar of the crowd was behind him. He was super, super nervous. But he'd done the work to live with the nerves.

'He wasn't playing Superman golf, he wasn't playing scared golf. He took his normal, relatively aggressive line – he played his normal golf.'

Cam went on to become number two in the world because he was able to keep playing his brand of golf, despite the nerves, not change it for the context of that particular game. In my own athletic career, the things that made me a promising recruit – my speed, a fairly aggressive play style, quick thinking on the field – were often out of my reach on game day as anxiety wore me down. These days, after a lot of growth, I'm better able to use my nerves as fuel, a fire that keeps me motivated rather than burning me up. Sometimes I wish those skills were something I'd started working on earlier in life, but I'm just grateful to have acquired them by this stage of the journey using the tools I've learned along the way.

Anxiety Toolkit

- Everyone feels anxious sometimes. It's easy for anxiety to get on top of you, but there are ways to manage it.
- Mental health is not the same as mental illness. Same as going to the gym to get your body fit, you can go to a therapist to train your mind.
- If you are feeling anxious about something, try taking deep breaths, or picturing a place you feel calm and safe.
- If those don't work, perhaps try Butters' option three: just get it done. At least, that's what worked for me in the cave and what you might be better off testing in a less stressful situation. You'll be amazed what you can achieve when it comes down to it.
- Competition is an ordinary performance on a special day. When you're faced with a challenge, don't deny the specialness of it. Embrace it.
- Nerves are the price of admission. It's normal to feel anxious around something that means a lot to you. A little anxiety is healthy – the price you pay to help reach your goals.
- Confidence and competence are different things. You can be good at what you do even if you don't feel confident on the day.

CHANGE

CHAPTER 5
WHEN ALL ELSE FAILS, PIVOT

I don't have any tattoos. Actually, that's not true – I've got a little toe-sleeve which was the result of a drunken night with the boys when my mate Hal Hunter, a tattoo artist, got his machine out. They should start putting breathalysers on those things, in all honesty. Anyway, if I was going to get a quote tattooed on my forehead, I know what it would say. There's a fair bit of room up there, so it could be a fairly long one, but this one is short, simple and absolutely true.

It's not what happens to you, it's how you react to it.

Not a new idea, but it's a good one. Pretty much more than anything, how you react to change determines what sort of a person you are. You can try as hard as you want, but you're never going to change the cards you were dealt. How you play them, though, is up to you.

I realise that's a bit of a strong statement and I'm wary of saying things are a certain way, because nine times out of ten, when you're *absolutely sure* about something you've said, you look back and go, *Oh my god, I was so wrong about that.* But that's why change is good. I don't have all the answers. But I can honestly say that the best things that ever happened to me came from failures and what came next.

I'd be lying if I said that being sacked by Carlton didn't hurt. I didn't much like what followed, either. Life was changing, not by my choice, but it was all happening anyway. Sometimes that's how it is. Once in a while life taps you on the shoulder and goes, 'What are you doing out there? Change it up, mate. Pick up the pace, or you're stuffed.'

It was more than a bit heartbreaking that my childhood dream of playing for the Blues had fallen apart. The club and I had parted on good terms, but I still had a lot of growing up to do. Honestly, when the dust settled, I thought I was done with footy for good. But then I got a call from Leon Cameron, coach at the GWS Giants, who invited me up to try out. So I flew up to Sydney, had the meeting with them, then flew back to Melbourne and waited on the call.

Eventually Leon called to let me know they weren't going to take me.

'Okay, that's cool,' I said. Then, it was like something came over me and I felt compelled to back myself. 'Nah, actually,

I reckon you should. You should pick me up. I think it's meant to happen.'

'Okay . . .' Leon paused. 'That's a bit weird, but whatever.'

I must have done something right because they ended up picking me up in the 2018 rookie draft and off I went to Sydney.

Being signed by the Giants was a lifeline. Honestly, in more ways than one. The glorious 300-game footy career I'd dreamt of wasn't on the cards, but I wasn't ready to be done with the game yet, either. I needed a chance to stretch my wings a bit, see how far I could fly if I actually left the nest.

When I got the sack from Carlton, even though I'd seen it coming, I didn't know what I was supposed to do next. I looked at my life and thought, *Shit, there's not that much going for me in this town*. Playing footy for Carlton had been my childhood dream. But since it had fallen over I'd gained a lot of perspective and I didn't necessarily love what I saw. I realised that I'd lived my whole life in and around Fitzroy, a circumference of the same five kilometres. I'd gone to the neighbourhood school, trained a kilometre away from the house and played for the team I'd grown up around. I'd known my friends all my life and while I love my mates, it's not good to go through life without meeting new people and having new experiences. My whole existence up until that point had been footy, and for all the amazing experiences the game gave me, it had also sheltered me from real life.

I'm not joking. Case in point – I didn't even know how to do my own laundry until I left Melbourne. It was just embarrassing. Whenever I'd play a game at Carlton I'd run out on to the field, play footy in front of the whole of Australia, then take my gear back to Mum's so she could wash off the grass, mud and blood. I was 26 years old and had only recently moved out of home with Juzz, thinking then was the smart time to buy a place and get a mortgage. And it would have been, if you don't count the fact I got the sack not long afterwards.

Luckily, the Giants signed me. I had no choice but to grow up, go somewhere else and do something different. My girlfriend (now beautiful wife) Juzz and I packed up and moved to Sydney.

Changing lanes

I knew I had to take a big step towards assuming responsibility for myself. Turns out that swapping teams while moving to a whole other city that I knew nothing about took that to a whole new level. The move happened so fast, we didn't even have a car up there. On day two I literally walked into a motorbike dealership and rode out on a scooter. I'd never seen myself as a scooter guy, but the minute I took it on the road it felt right. Only a little bike, but it had guts, and there's nothing like fanging around Sydney on a motorbike. I never would have known that if I hadn't taken a chance.

I'd never lived in a rental, so had no idea about leases or bonds or any of it, but we found a nice little house in Paddington that was perfect. Or it seemed perfect. A month in we realised it was falling apart. Two months in we realised that we couldn't actually afford to live there. I was on AFL rookie wages, which weren't bad, but Sydney rents are crazy. My salary didn't stretch to the cost of living. But then, right around the time I was really scratching my head trying to figure out how I was going to pay the rent, a mate of mine, Jake, called up.

'Dyl, I'm moving to Sydney,' Jake said. 'Do you know anyone who's got a room?'

'Yes, actually. Come move in with me.'

He did and we're best mates to this day. Living together was great – he made the time I spent in Sydney so amazing. It was a lucky situation, but I'm aware our friendship probably wouldn't have got to the level it did if we hadn't lived together out of necessity. If I hadn't jumped in the deep end, financially speaking, and needed someone to help cover rent, then my missus, mate and I would never have shared that incredible experience.

It was a time of real change. I loved my new gig at the Giants, but my footy still wasn't setting the world on fire. Things weren't going well for me, through no fault of the club. I was injured more often than not and my best on-field years were clearly behind me. It was tough because I've had a lot of injuries over my career, but a lot of them were clean, predicable hurts: a broken bone or a shoulder or something that can be repaired with surgery or a clearly defined rehab routine. But it had gotten to the stage where I'd done my fourth or fifth calf strain for the year. And with a calf strain you just don't know when it's going to straighten itself out, or even specifically what caused it. It's not a direct impact injury with a clear path to recovery. Once you've had a few of them you lose absolute confidence in your body.

It was becoming pretty clear that my footy was going one way and my future the other. I had to work out what I was going to do for a living when it wrapped up. I was determined not to get caught on the back foot again and find myself wondering what the fuck I was going to do with my life. I'd been worrying about this as I rode my scooter home and somewhere along the way, things started to get a little clearer. As I was walking back to the house, it hit me out of the blue: the way I chose to perceive my looming delisting was entirely up to me.

This thing, the end of my footy . . . it was going to happen and I was fine with it. More than fine, I was excited. Getting let go by the Giants wasn't something I could control, but my reaction to it would be. Maybe it wouldn't be a loss at all, but a gained opportunity – freedom to prioritise whatever came next without worrying about letting a team down. That's when I realised how far I'd come since the last time I'd been dropped. I felt like a much better person. When I was sacked by Carlton, I'd seen it as a loss. This time I saw it as an opportunity to change.

In that moment, climbing off my scooter, I realised that gratitude had started to alter who I was as a person. My entire mindset was different. I'd changed. That's a good thing. One thing I really believe is that change is good. It can be confronting. It can be scary. Often it makes you shit-scared.

> *One thing I really believe is that change is good. It can be confronting. It can be scary. Often it makes you shit-scared. But change is an opportunity to react in a positive way.*

But change is an opportunity to react in a positive way.

Because I knew what was going to happen, and completely accepted it, for the rest of the year I came in with the best attitude, the biggest smile and just really loved and enjoyed my last days as an AFL player. Every time I walked into the gym, I was like, *Well, I'm not gonna be doing this much longer. So let's enjoy it.* When I think about that time, I don't remember being stressed about money, or weighed down with responsibility, or being down in the dumps that playing for the Giants wasn't exactly working out. I remember the exhilaration of taking risks and not knowing what was coming next.

This one moment stands out in my mind. I was on my scooter, riding across the Harbour Bridge. In whichever direction I turned my head there was a beautiful harbour stretching out forever. I'll never forget that feeling. It was like living in a movie. The world spun around us and Juzz, Jake and I embraced this new way of living. From that run-down house in Paddington, I'd head down to the beach every day and get in the ocean. It was almost like a meditation for me. I'd dive under a wave and feel it break over my head, go down my back, my legs, my feet – as if the water was washing away all my stress and bad energy. I've never met a bad mood that four or five waves down at Bronte couldn't fix.

Not to get too philosophical, but I really do believe that if you dive in and show willing then the world will work with you. Yes, it can be stressful, but you've got to make the first move so that other things can get onboard. Then ride the wave and use its power to your advantage. In the end, it's not what happens but how you react to it and what you can learn from it to take you to the next thing.

Turns out the next thing was a bit of a surprise, even to me.

Big life questions: what the fuck is a podcast?

That Christmas, 2017, I travelled over to Western Australia for Christmas with the family. Over lunch my cousin and I started talking about true crime, a genre I've always been into.

'If you like true crime stories,' she told me, 'you've got to check out this podcast.'

'OK, yep, absolutely,' I said. 'But what the fuck is a podcast?'

'It's sort of like an audiobook, it tells a whole story . . .'

'Mate. That sounds boring.'

'It's sick. Trust me.' And she kept at it until I downloaded *Serial* – that first super-massive true crime podcast that kick-started the whole industry, pretty much. Everyone loved it. Me included, I binged the whole thing. It was just magic. Never experienced anything like it.

On the plane back to Sydney, I was listening to podcasts and thinking things over and started to get the spark of an idea that it might be cool to get into radio. I'd dabbled with media production here and there while at Carlton, largely thanks to my mate, Luca Gonano. Luca was the head of media for Carlton in my final years and a good mate of mine.

He and I got along really well and I would often find myself sitting around Princes Park having a banter with him. One day he asked me if I wanted to do a show. It would be called *Discussions with Dylan*, he said, and I'd get teammates on just to talk to them, have a bit of banter.

'No way,' I said.

He kept asking, and I kept saying no. Until after about the 1000th time, when I finally agreed. I'd always loved getting to know people, connecting on a bit of a deeper level and just talking to the guys. I had good relationships with all the players and Luca must have thought I'd be a good person to try and do it, so we got out a camera and started up our little show. I wish I could tell you he could see the talent shining out of me, but to be honest, I was the only one up for the gig – no one else wanted to do it. Back in the day, doing media stuff was sort of frowned upon. I copped a lot of shit from everyone for doing it, actually, but I ended up really enjoying it. Getting on camera, having fun. I remember thinking, *You know, if this is a career path, I'd love to take it.*

So I'd always had this idea sort of rattling around the back of my mind, that one day, after my AFL career was done, I'd walk into a job at a commercial broadcaster. Turns out, that wasn't on the cards. My AFL career wasn't as glory-filled as it might have been, so I wasn't exactly fighting off sponsors and TV stations with a pointy stick. My pitch would basically have been, 'I'm on a contract with the GWS Giants right now, but my career is in the toilet and I'm probably not going to be playing for long.' I would have been laughed out of the room. I had no real experience, nothing to show for myself.

But I started to make little moves. I got a part time job at Triple M in Sydney, one day a week, when I didn't need to be at footy. Very basic stuff, answering phones and sort of absorbing everything I could about how a radio show is put together. I'd ride my scooter into the city, then go in and try and make myself useful and learn what I could.

The idea, eventually, was to start a podcast. There's obviously a lot of reasons why I started it, but the main one is because I had nothing really to show for myself as a radio guy. I had no other way to get into a career that I wanted. I figured that if I started a podcast, I'd have something to show for myself when my footy was over. When I'd left Carlton, I'd had absolutely nothing. This time, I wanted something in my back pocket for when my time with the Giants ended. If it only lasted for twelve months, I could at least say, 'I made this podcast. It's a bit rough, but I've interviewed a few guys and I know my way around a microphone, so don't be scared to give me a chance.' That was the initial goal. Just to give myself a bit of a calling card to get into radio.

Pretty soon I was spending maybe 80 per cent of my time at the Giants, the other 20 learning how to make a pod. My mate Ryan Miller, an absolute gun in the AFL media unit and all-round legend, took me under his wing and showed me the ropes – how to actually record decent sound, upload it, edit it and put it together so it tells a story – all that basic stuff I had no idea about. I'd never really worked with a laptop before, so I was going in blind.

I can't say I planned it very well. I decided the pod would be called *Dyl & Friends*, and basically it was just going to be me and some of the footy boys having a bit of a banter. That was about the extent of the business plan. The first episode went up in July 2018. Geez it was ordinary. When I listen back to those first episodes they make me wince. Sometimes I have to fight the urge to delete them. But at the same time, I'm actually sort of proud of them, because they show how far we've come.

There's a really great bit of advice I heard: 'If you start a new business and you're not embarrassed by it, you started too late.' I think that's spot on, it really hits home for me. Sure, those first episodes are a bit cringe, but letting embarrassment hold me back wasn't an option. I chased every opportunity to grow the pod, including hitting up AFL marketing to see if they wanted to collaborate or find a sponsor. By 2019, I was rocking up to GWS pressers in my street clothes and interviewing my own team as 'Dylan from *Dyl & Friends*'. My friends – in life there is no glory without a bit of cringe.

But it's been incredible, the journey. Gee-whiz, I've learned a lot. It started as a bit of a joke and whatnot, but the second I started to take myself seriously, so did the rest of the world.

When I was a younger guy, I used to base my decisions on the people around me and what they did. I'd constantly be looking for reassurance from others that I was making the right choices – for justification to support whatever it was I was doing – and it really dictated the actions I took. But then I realised how crazy it was to be outsourcing my ambition to people who didn't necessarily share my dream.

The thing is, negativity is an infinite resource. There was always someone waiting to give me grief for wanting to try something and really putting my balls on the line. I said to myself, *I can't keep listening to what everyone else is telling me.* There were so many things I wanted to do and it was time to just commit to doing them – things like starting the podcast. From there, instead of giving people the option to talk me out of my plans, I started to act with intention.

The thing is, negativity is an infinite resource.

'I'm doing X,' I would tell them and say it like I meant it. I've found when you voice an intention with conviction people just get out of your way because they think, *Oh, this person really knows exactly what they're doing.*

I like the analogy of being stuck in heavy traffic – an idea that struck me as I was driving to work, battling the logjam of Punt Road's peak-hour traffic. Like everyone from Melbourne, I've spent a fair amount of my life crawling up and down Punt. So let's imagine I'm with you in the passenger seat and you're driving down Punt's middle lane, stuck in traffic, but you realise you need to turn left. So, you turn on your indicator signalling you need to go left and . . . nothing. It's Punt Road. Everyone is stressed out and rushing to where they need to be. Nobody cares that you're in the wrong lane. You can sit there all day with your indicator blinking, but not moving. But if you put your indicator on, look behind you and start edging into their lane like you mean it, it's amazing how the cars will make space and let you in. They think, *This person knows where they're going, they want to turn left, let's let them in.* And before you know it, you're on your way. So that's how I like to make my decisions these days. It's a real game-changer.

My delisting from Carlton and the lifeline the Giants threw me turned out to be the motivation I needed. It was time for me start moving out of the lane I was stuck in. I turned on my blinker and I went from there. I started *Dyl & Friends*, really, just sitting down with a couple of mates and a microphone and no idea what we were doing. But we did it with conviction.

I started from scratch – learned how to record audio, how to edit a conversation, how to produce a show and put it all together. It's incredible how much I've had to learn. How many times I've been humbled and knocked down and had to be pulled up by my mates who gave me support and held me accountable. After a life where I'd been handed opportunity after opportunity, I suddenly found myself without a clear path. I had to make my own way. Out of everything I learned, the biggest takeaway was that being thrown a curveball and having to think on my feet is an amazing gift.

Boys, it was bloody fantastic

Sure enough, in due time Leon called me into his office and let me know I was going to be delisted for the second time. Which is a bit of an achievement on my behalf, I reckon. Lots of players get delisted. But twice in a few years? That's making history, my friends.

So I had a really good chat with Leon and he was awesome about it all. In the end we hugged and after a couple of wonderful years with the Giants, my AFL dream was done. It's funny, because although I will always love footy and it was a childhood dream, by that point, after my epiphany on the scooter, I was really hoping that things would fall the way they did. If I'd been offered another year of footy it would have held me back from throwing everything I had at my new dream. Because I lost the safety net, I had no choice but to succeed in my new vocation. In all honesty, I was absolutely ecstatic to finish up.

One of the hardest parts of that second delisting was saying goodbye to the boys. You do all the formal parts of delisting: exit interview, media, all of that, but the kicker was leaving the club WhatsApp group. The group chat at any club is fantastic and gee we had some banter! Some truly epic times. Especially over the last month we'd been sending in some very, very funny material and, not to brag, but for the record, most of it was mine. My footy may have been going south all that year, but believe me, my meme game was strong; I scored many, many goals on that front. Really, I felt sorry for the lads who were going to miss out when I was off the team.

So, for that, leaving the group sucked. I mean, it *really* hurt. I'd woken up after a goodbye celebration with the boys where I'd had a few brown cordials too many, a little bit hungover, a little bit sad, and thought, *Gee, maybe it's time to send the boys a message and get out of there.* So, I did. 'Boys, it's been bloody fantastic. Thanks so much for everything. I'll always be there if you need me.'

I would miss the boys. God, I would miss the football club. In hindsight, is it sad that the only things I miss about footy are the banter and locker room? Not really, it was pretty funny. Nah, I wasn't sad about it. More than anything, I couldn't wait to see what I would make of myself.

CHAPTER 6
THE MYTH OF THE SELF-MADE MAN

Think about the idea of the 'self-made man'. When I was younger, I wanted to be that. I once saw this guy who was very successful, very cool, who had this big tattoo across his torso that read 'Self-Made,' and I thought, *That's cool. That's what I want to be. I want to be self-made.*

I've had the opportunity to chat to many 'self-made' men and women on the pod and they've all had something in common. They are successful not because they've had it easy, but because they made the choice to react positively to the hard times. One of my all-time favourite chats on the pod was with Christian O'Connell, the broadcast and podcast legend.[7] These days he's the voice of Gold 104.3's nationally syndicated radio breakfast show and one of Australia's best loved talkback hosts. How he got there is a story that's as funny as it is inspiring. I've got a lot from Christian because he's managed to create an amazing career for himself twice over, out of nothing but his own drive. No contacts, no privilege, just sheer grit and being the nicest guy on the planet.

Christian grew up in the small English city of Winchester, about 90 minutes out of London. To him, the town was peaceful and quiet. Too peaceful and quiet.

'I couldn't wait to get out of there,' he says. 'I had dreams of doing stand-up and radio and I got that bug at a very young age.'

He remembers being about 13 years old, watching TV with his parents, when Scottish comedian Billy Connolly came on. His parents, a nurse and a factory worker who 'worked proper jobs', started absolutely losing it, rolling on the floor helpless with laughter.

'I'd never seen them laugh like that,' says Christian. 'Just from hearing Billy Connolly talk about life and telling stories. The power of that. What a magical thing to do.'

Around the same time, Christian started listening to a radio DJ and comedian with an edgy, subversive vibe and got hooked. From then, he knew he wanted a career in media, but had no idea how to get one. How was he going to get from his tiny little house in Winchester onto the radio?

'I had no idea. There was no path ahead of me. My mum and dad weren't in that kind of industry.'

He found it by working his way up from a sales job for a British media company, getting to know the bosses, getting an audition, to finally, a stint on the airwaves. It meant taking a 60 per cent pay cut and came with a very good chance that he'd never make a living. But he did it anyway.

That led to a 20-year career in the UK, where he eventually became one of London's most popular radio personalities. Then, in 2018, at the height of his fame, a family holiday to Australia prompted him to packed it all in to move across the world and start again with a breakfast show on Aussie radio. It basically meant starting from zero; a huge risk that didn't immediately pay off. In those early days, Christian felt the very distinct possibility of getting sacked. 'It turned out that Australians did not want to hear an English guy that early on in the day. They fucking hated me.'

He remembers going for a pint at a pub on a Friday evening and being approached by someone he assumed was a fan who'd recognised him and wanted to say hello.

'Are you the bloke from the radio?' the guy asked.

Christian smiled and held out a hand.

The guy just sniffed. 'Not going very well, is it?'

But Christian didn't give up. He kept making moves and when Covid came along just as his career was taking off again, he reacted like he always had. Every time he'd been knocked down, lost an opportunity, or been sacked, he'd held firm to the belief that it was leading him somewhere he needed to be.

'You look at these zigzags – and you can only see them looking back, you don't see it at the time,' Christian says, 'but, you join the dots and you realise, *Okay, actually I was right where I needed to be.*'

When Christian told me that, he put his finger on something I'd recently been getting my head around. There have been many times in life when I've felt like I'm banging my head against the wall. Working my arse off to try and achieve a certain result, only to fall short for one reason or another. But I'd begun to notice that all those times when things had gone a bit shit for me, they'd ended up good in the long run. Not like they were 'destined to happen', or any woo-woo stuff like that, but simply that they'd happened, so I'd had to react to them and that had led to me where I'd needed to go.

Christian and I hit it off, I think, because we both like to get to a deeper level in our chats – the real stuff, the raw stuff, the tender stuff. I love talking to people about the struggles they've had in their life. Because whatever struggle you've had, and some people have had awful struggles, there would've been a gift in it. In that darkness, there's a gift – it changes who you are in that moment.

In our interview, Christian shared a saying that he continues to find strength in. 'This too shall pass.' It means that no matter how hard or bloody amazing the moment you find yourself currently in, that moment is going to end. It'll be over soon, and another, different moment is already on the way. So, stay on the ride.

Change is inevitable, so you may as well make the most of it. When things are tough it's difficult to believe that the hardship will ever end. But it will. And you'll become a different person through the process. That's how Christian O'Connell and so many success stories I've been lucky to hear all get to where they're going. They embrace the change and push on to better things. Because life is nothing but an endless stream of change.

Life is five per cent what happens to you and 95 per cent what you do with it. I mean, you can try to fight it, but honestly – you don't have a choice in the matter. One second you're 16 and a promising footy player, the next you're about to turn 30 and your knees are like, 'Sorry, I'm leaving the group chat.'

Life is five per cent what happens to you and 95 per cent what you do with it.

Life is about the big moments, sure – they're what we remember and how we tell the stories of our lives. But those big crucible moments comprise an infinite number of smaller moments. The big shifts – getting sacked, the move to Sydney, getting sacked again – are made up of thousands of smaller, micro moments that are constantly coming at you. Fumbling a ball in a preliminary match, taking the afternoon off to enjoy the sunshine, getting coffee with a new mate, dodging the wrong way on the field and straight into the opposing team's biggest lad – all opportunities for change.

Learning to love adversity

In those moments of adversity when there's hardship and you're really stressed . . . I've also found beauty. Those moments simplify your life. You can have a million things going on, but when a crisis point arrives it crystallises what's most important to you. You tell yourself, *This is what's happening. This is what I need to do.*

There's this metaphor I love. It's a bit cringe, but all the best ones are, so here it is.

When you're at your lowest, kicked down by life, it's very dark. It can feel like being suffocated. But how you choose to experience those times is up to you. You can think of yourself as being buried in dirt, or you can think of yourself as a seed in soil about to sprout. All that shit and dirt and weight that's being piled on top of you? It isn't there to hold you down, it's fertiliser to help you grow. While you're down there beneath the earth, you start sprouting roots and they spread like a support network. When you finally shoot through the dirt those roots give you the strength you need to stand tall. It's going to be really fucking hard to knock you over because you have this network of strength beneath you, holding you firm.

Getting off the bench

I tried to get some work in radio, but nothing was really happening. Still, I was trying to be proactive. Me and Juzz packed up our Sydney lives, went back to Melbourne and I put the word out that I wanted to work in media. And . . . crickets. I had some meetings with a few places, but nobody really wanted me to work for them. 3AW were the exception. They are one of the biggest radio stations in Melbourne and when I moved back home, they gave me a shot.

It meant starting at the very bottom, a casual part-time entry level gig that paid $27 bucks an hour – a huge step-down from what I'd made as an AFL player, obviously. A bit of a drop in status as well. I remember going in my first week expecting this hero's welcome. 'Here's someone who's played footy for eight years, what a great addition to our organisation,' I imagined them saying. 'And we get you for $27 bucks an hour? We're rapt.'

Surprise – nothing like that occurred. The complete opposite, actually. My first assignment was sitting in on a breakfast show. For two days I sat behind this huge analogue control panel and said nothing, wasn't allowed to speak. The one time I tried to say something and contribute to the production of the show, I got shushed by the executive producer. My only task was to go downstairs and pick up lunch for everybody and bring it back up to the studio. I remember being in the elevator with my arms full of sandwiches and water bottles and thinking, 'What the fuck am I doing here?' I felt like I deserved more respect, but in truth, I hadn't done the work to earn it yet. So that was an important lesson.

During the early days of my career transition, the hardest part of embracing new things was dropping my ego. Each new shift felt like a demotion. It was a real knock to my pride to go from being an AFL star rookie being cheered by crowds of diehard fans, to being knocked back to the reserves bench on another team, to finally, shafted to the lowest rung in an office environment where nobody gave a shit about any of my previous achievements. One minute I was up on a pedestal, the next I was making minimum wage while collecting lunches for people years younger than me who had more authority, respect and shitload higher salaries. It was a humbling experience, that's for sure. But it's good to be humbled. I know now that I needed to be humbled.

The upside of ego

If you take a big swing and miss, that's fine – you learn from it and you move on. At the same time, it's important to take the time to appreciate your achievements – because you worked hard to get there and you should celebrate that. It's the thrill of success and ambition that keeps you working.

There was a saying that Carlton coach Mick Malthouse used to roll out when talking about ego and entitlement: *Too much water, you drown. Not enough water, you die of thirst. But somewhere in the middle is the level of water you need to live.*

Ego is a bit like that. You've got to find a healthy level to fuel yourself without managing to lodge your head up your own arse.

Working in radio was such a great equaliser for me. It really drove home the realisation that nobody owed me anything. More to the point, I was a nobody. If I was going to make a name for myself in the media world I was going to have to start again from scratch, put in the hard yards and keep going. And I learned a lot. I got to work with some really good people on the control desk for the likes of Tom Elliot, Rex Hunt and Dee Dee Dunleavy.

My job was entry-level producer stuff – answering the phones and finding callers to put through. I'd answer a call, suss out whether the person would be good 'talent' for a chat with the hosts, get an idea of what they wanted to say, and if they passed muster, patch them through live on air along with a message to the hosts, so they could pick up the conversation.

Problem was, I had no real interest. The topics being discussed, the themes of the shows, none of it was stuff I was passionate about. Once I got a handle on the technical stuff, I stopped giving it 100 per cent of my attention and soon I was phoning it in. Literally. It reached a point where I was just putting callers through without doing my due diligence; not properly vetting the calls to see if they were good talent, or even whether they'd meant to call the show.

There was one time where someone had dialled the wrong number, looking for an Auto Tune mechanic. This happened quite a bit because the number for the studio and the number for Auto Tune were almost identical. But this one time the phones were going nuts and I wasn't really paying attention, so I put this guy looking for a mechanic straight through, live on air. Suddenly the hosts and entire listening audience were copping an earful from this guy about an oil change. By some luck the segment was about cars, so the hosts could wing it and it wasn't so bad. But then I did it again. And again. The third time it happened was on the afternoon show during the middle of a discussion about laundry and stain removal tips. The caller wanted help with their car.

That was the final straw. I got sacked from that job too, faster than usual. So three sackings in three years – surely some kind of record. When I first left, I spoke really negatively of the experience, which I regret now. With time, I realised that being let go was for the best. I returned to my mantra – it wasn't my sacking that mattered, but how I reacted to it. I didn't love my time in commercial radio, but what an awesome first-hand experience in learning that I never wanted to work in that field ever again. If I had loved it, even if I'd been a little bit content, I probably wouldn't have been motivated to start my own business.

What a blessing to have seen that potential life up close and realised, *Nah thanks, not for me*. That style of radio producer – the people I met who were running those shows – were role models of a sort; ones that taught me exactly what I *didn't* want to do. In its own way it inspired me to go on and do something different. Which I feel so grateful for.

I think that anyone, but especially young people who are still trying to figure it all out, can get a lot out of those so-called 'bad' experiences. Shit jobs, bad relationships. Take them as they are: lessons on what direction to take – not this one! You can take so much from the bad times if you're willing to look at them from a new point of view. I chose to see my sacking from 3AW as an opportunity to fully commit to my own production and see what I could make of myself.

Lucky for me, I had a champion in my corner: Adam Baldwin. I'd actively sought out Adam as a bit of a mentor when I realised my footy career was coming to a close as I'd seen other mates struggle with the transition from AFL to the 'real world'. I'd gone from high school straight into the AFL, so until the age of 27, everything in my life had been scheduled and managed by other people. I knew I'd need some help on the other side.

From the get-go, Adam backed me. As Head of Communications in the AFL Players' Association, Adam knew a lot – about business things and life in general – that I needed to get up to speed on. Things like organising my life, scheduling my diary (which I do in detail to this day) and setting goals outside the footy arena. We met every Wednesday for two years through Covid and he sorted me out, always looking for ways to help me succeed. I'm forever in debt to his love and guidance both then and now.

And so is our business. These days, Producey is a decent-sized media production company operating out of Melbourne. But we started small, with Adam looking at the business side, Sam Bosner on production, and me behind the mic, all having a crack just to see what (if anything) we could make from it all. We played around, tested out this and that, but when I left 3AW we took a real swing and opened our first studio.

For $100 a week we rented a room above a deli in Albert Park. A tiny place where you could hear the trams rattling down to the beach and smell the burger place across the road when you opened the windows. It was a huge amount of money at the time. The minute we put money down, I started worrying about how we could afford it.

None of us (me least of all) had any real idea what we were doing, so we just started making moves, and once we were doing production full time, there was no other way but forward. We had no choice but to keep going as hard as we could. We started getting sponsors involved and then colleagues started to come onboard and Sam levelled up our production game exponentially. He was cut from the same kind of cloth as me – ambitious, loved pods – and basically signed up to work for nothing but belief in our potential.

We started the business completely the opposite way from how it's supposed to be done – with just an idea, really, just coming up with the name: Producey. I thought it was so sick, but surely it would be taken. My first prerequisite was the name. Second was going to Instagram and nabbing the handle. Third was being able to register it as a website. It wasn't cheap, not something we could afford easily, but I've always been pretty impulsive and it felt like it had to happen. So it did.

With all our chips stacked on Producey, we went from there. We got another editor, then before we knew it, found ourselves paying full-time staff and realising we had the skills and the ambition to produce a variety of podcasts beyond *Dyl & Friends*. Next minute we'd acquired a studio space in Richmond with our name on the door and found ourselves walking into this big echoing studio space, like, 'Fuck, that escalated.'

We built it all out of nothing. But we didn't do it alone. From Adam, Sam and me in the beginning, Producey is now an awesome team of people I love working with every day, that now also includes Zach, Darcy, Scott, Sam D and Stef. And of course, Dan with *List Cloggers*, and all the other creators we work with who've also becomes mates, many who contributed to this book. After my actual family, you guys are my family – the reason I come to work every day, but also why I'm living my best life. Bloody legends, the lot of ya.

Not every goal has to land to be a win

Let's go back to the idea of the self-made man and how that applies to change. Alongside seeing a bit of success making podcasts and building my business I've been getting my life together. I've done some things I've been really proud of, but ultimately, I realise that I'm the *furthest thing possible* from a self-made man.

I don't think anyone is, to be honest. Even people who think they're self-made – that they've reached a certain place in life by doing it all on their own – chances are they probably didn't. Not unless they grew up on Mars.

It's impossible to live on Earth and not be affected by others. We are made from our experiences – all the positive and negative things that happen to us. If you're successful in life it might be because you had good parents, solid mates around you to support you, or resources to tap when you hit a roadblock. It's equally true that your success might come from having had none of these things; not necessarily assistance, but resistance. It's ironic, but I've often found that negative experiences deliver the most positive results. Even if it doesn't feel like it at the time.

Take this story, for instance. If there's one thing my footy mates know about me, it's that I love a win. There's nothing better than a goal. It's a great feeling – you snap the ball off the foot, get the goal, get the glory, hear the roar of the crowd. All the good things in life. So, picture me . . .

In this particular game, I'm on the ground at the 'G, my second home, absolutely tearing it up. I'm racing up the field with big Joe Daniher chasing me and have no fear. I shrug him off, bang the ball straight flush towards the goal and turn around and start celebrating. I'm giving it to the stadium, the punters are going bananas. It feels so good. I am roaring, cheering with the crowd, until one of the lads pulls me up and tells me to get my head back in the game. Soon as I do, I realise I've counted my chickens before they've hatched. Missed the goal, as it turns out.

Sheesh, it felt bad in the moment, but I don't think it really hits me until afterwards when one of the boys says to me, 'Mate, that's so embarrassing.'

I picture my silly noggin streaming across everyone's TVs. 'Yeah, shit. That's gonna be everywhere.'

And it was. There was a lot of good footy played that day, but my carrying on like an absolute peanut was all over the TV, the papers, the internet. I was mortified.

Later on, looking back on that incident, I realised I'd been looking at it the wrong way. By then I'd learned to flip the script, find the positive and had finally begun to understand it all a bit better. You don't need to let setbacks, struggles, or embarrassingly public missed goals get you down. You can take a lot more from the negative experiences than you do from positive ones. That moment taught me to keep my head where my body's at – not get ahead of the game.

It also became an early lesson on reframing towards the positive. That's what real strength is. That's how you make a man.

Change Toolkit

- Change is inevitable, so you may as well enjoy it.
- Put your intentions out into the world. If you're changing lanes in traffic, nobody is going to let you in unless you put your blinker on and drive like you mean it.
- Every challenge is a chance for you to grow. Being sacked felt like a failure, but it was actually an amazing opportunity.
- Feeling grateful activates the part of your brain associated with grit and determination. Think of some things you are grateful for and take the time to appreciate them. Write down a list. Practise gratitude regularly to make it a habit.
- When you feel like you're being buried by stress, think again. Don't think you're being buried, but that you're a seed waiting to grow.
- Ego is not a bad thing. It's like water – too much and you'll drown, not enough and you'll die of thirst.
- Failure is not something to be ashamed of. Every setback is a chance to try new things until you get it right.
- There's no such thing as a 'self-made man'. You are the sum of all the things that have happened to you, good and bad. Those experiences are what make you.

FRIENDSHIP

CHAPTER 7

TO SEE THE FUTURE, LOOK AT YOUR MATES

The older I get the more I appreciate just how lucky I am to have known so many champions growing up. In many ways, you are the sum of the people you surround yourself with; they have an undeniably huge impact on your life. What your tribe says, does and thinks, and what they encourage *you* to say and think – it matters. It really matters. There's that saying, 'Show me your best friends and I'll show you your future.' It's true.

Changing cities, footy clubs and careers, and the interesting people I met along the way, really opened my eyes to what a lucky start I'd had. I was blessed to grow up with some awesome mates who were good influences on me. I've done a lot of reflecting on that time. I really think I lucked into a good mix of loyalty and respect, with enough risk-taking that we never stood still.

As kids, we were all super competitive and into pushing boundaries. I think we learned a lot from growing up the way we did, going out and doing dumb shit in the Fitzroy area. A bit of tagging, a bit of egging houses, a bit of booze, all the good stuff – risky teenage stupidity, which I don't condone and which I'm not going to go into too much here because my mum's going to read this. There was definitely a period there where I went through a bit of a wild stage. Luckily, the mates I did it with were fundamentally awesome. We encouraged each other to push boundaries, but at the same time, looked out for each other.

Way back in the juniors, we were taught by a coach that no matter what happens, you never leave your mates behind. It's one of those early lessons that seems innocuous and simple when you first hear it, but has stuck with me all through the years. Because of it, we've always pushed each other in a positive direction and will always be committed to each other. All growing up we had each other's backs, supporting each other in hard times and encouraging each other towards becoming better people.

We've all had our challenges, but as we head into our thirties, we're all pretty happy in life – mad fucking go-getters that just push each other to the limit. At all times, always. When we were playing footy, or mucking about, or starting our careers, we were never satisfied – we were always looking towards kicking the next goal. What's next to do? We were drawn to each other because we were already super competitive and lucky we found each other, I guess. Those guys have pushed me harder and I've pushed them. I'm not surprised that we've all done well.

Driven people drive you to be better

You might have heard the idea that 'no man is an island'. It's a bit of wisdom that's lasted for centuries because it's true: none of us exists separate to others. When we understand ourselves in connection with our mates and the people we love, our world expands. You can't do that when you're isolated.

When we understand ourselves in connection with our mates and the people we love, our world expands.

At a certain point, I suppose, I neglected the importance of true connection and started making friendships that didn't nourish me on a deeper level. As my footy career progressed and I started making new mates I found it safer to hide my vulnerable side. Because we all came from different backgrounds, the rules were different. I guess it felt safer to play by their rules and adapt to the banter and language of the new group, than to live authentically.

Somewhere along the line, that turned into me becoming a negative person. On reflection, I think that's partly because I'd let myself become a bit of an island. I'd become really removed from who I truly was as a person. So, no wonder I came unstuck. Humans aren't meant to be islands. Truth is, we're more like cities. We're social creatures. We understand each other by who we associate with.

I'd grown up with driven people, who'd driven me to be better, but somehow, I'd stopped. Until Bolts shook me out of my negative mindset that day in 2016, I didn't realise how far I'd fallen out of touch with myself. I hadn't realised who I'd let move into my mental city, so to speak. Since then, I've always made the time to take check of situations and note who's around me – in good times and bad.

You've probably done this instinctively yourself in bad times. When things go wrong in life and things are shit, it's natural to look around for someone else to blame. We've all been guilty of fucking things up and looking for some explanation beyond our own actions. But how often do you do that when things are good? Who's around you then? Are good things happening in your life purely out of luck? Or your own actions?

To use a bit of a footy analogy, life is a team sport. On the AFL field, while it goes without saying that the most important and beloved player on the field is the humble midfielder, that's just one position on the field. It takes a whole team working as a unit to get the ball up the field and through the sticks. So, when good things happen in your life, take the time to look around and really take in who you've got around you. Are the goals you're kicking, so to speak, happening because there's a whole team of people around you that are pitching in?

A big part of making sure you're surrounding yourself with good people is to ask yourself why they are your mates. Why do you like them? And more importantly, why do they like you?

Being liked versus being respected

When I was younger, all I wanted was to be liked by everyone. Right through life – from primary school, to high school, to the AFL – I just wanted to hang out and be everyone's friend. I never really stopped to examine that until I learned the difference between wanting to be liked for the way I acted and wanting to be respected for who I am.

As a young 18-year-old kid, coming straight from school to join an AFL club, there were all these behaviours I picked up purely because I thought that's what men do, so that's what I would do to get people to like me. Because if everyone liked me, then nobody would give me shit.

At school, I thought, *Well, I'm a guy, this is what I have to do: I have to play footy, I have to hang out with cool kids and try to talk to girls to be cool.*

Then when I got to into footy, I was like, *I'm a footy player now. And footy players are LADS. They gamble. That's cool. Okay, I'm gonna start gambling. They go clubbing. Alright, sweet, I'll start going clubbing.*

It took me probably two or three years, honestly, to work out, *Fuck man, I really don't like any of these things.* To realise I'd been jumping through all these hoops to try and fit in, when realistically, I was never going to fit that mould. Putting on a fancy outfit and going to see a DJ wasn't fun for me. I love torch songs. Big chords, big feelings. Huge sad songs. But I would never tell anyone that because I was afraid that they'd take the piss out of me.

Who would *you* call when the shit hits the fan?

I remember being away on a trip in my second year at Carlton and talking with Darren Harris, our development coach. Darren asked me who on the team I'd take to war with me.

'What do you mean?'

'If you had to go to war,' he said, 'Who would you bring with you?'

That was interesting. I'd never considered the concept before, but after a minute or two I gave him the names of three of my closest friends at the club.

'Do you reckon those guys are the best choice to back you up? If you were in the trenches and people were shooting at you, would you trust them to save your life?'

'Fuck,' I said, 'I don't know.'

I realised that, actually, if I were being honest, those probably weren't the guys I would choose to have by my side in a life-or-death situation. I'd probably choose some of the more senior guys. There were a couple of salty old blokes at Carlton who I don't think would blink if you threw a grenade at them. Those were the guys you'd want around if your back was up against the wall.

It's not that the guys I was hanging out with were bad people. They were some of the nicest guys you'd ever meet. I hung out with them because they were heaps of fun and the banter was premium. But what I was getting from their friendship was not compatible with the self-image I wanted as a professional footballer.

That was a really big moment for me, really got me in the

guts. Not so much that my closest mates at the club weren't legends. Just that I wouldn't necessarily trust them to take a bullet for me.

It hit me even harder when Darren asked, 'Now, would anyone want to go to war with you?'

I knew that people liked me, but did they think I was the sort of person they could turn to when the shit hit the fan? I didn't know, but the longer I thought about it, the more uneasy I felt. It was a hard realisation to accept that if people were having a shit time, they probably wouldn't trust me to be there for them.

Real mates have each other's backs

When I was a kid I watched *Bra Boys*, the 2007 documentary about the surf gang based in Maroubra, Sydney.[8] Obviously I don't condone violence or gang activity or any of that stuff the Bra Boys are famous for, but their spirit of loyalty stuck with me. The idea that brotherhood is not about mates having your back, but about *you having theirs*. There's more pride in being the guy your mates would turn to in a crisis than being the most popular guy in the room. It's one thing to know that people will support you, but the big question in life is, will you support them? Are you someone capable of supporting others, who can help others through the hard times?

It's one thing to know that people will support you, but the big question in life is, will you support them?

It took me a while to realise that when adversity comes, people don't turn to the people they like, necessarily. They turn to the ones they know will help them, who will be honest with them and give them the support they need. People don't want to be told that they're killing it. They want help navigating the tough situations from someone who knows what they're doing.

That conversation with Darren about war mates was the start of a lot of realisations for me. Later on, as the podcast started to evolve from a sports-and-banter sort of thing into exploring areas of mental health and vulnerability, the ideas it raised led to a lot of very real conversations with mates, friends and family. Because I turned up to my interviews with full-on honest vulnerability, it opened the gates for people to be vulnerable with me when they were struggling. I knew my mates liked hanging out with me, but I began to realise that I wanted to be the person they could rely on. Being that person is so rewarding.

Admittedly, it's been a bit of a journey to get here. I'm the first to admit that I haven't always been a standout in those situations. My mate and *List Cloggers* co-host, Dan Gorringe, and I had to work through a fair bit of the old toxic masculinity before we reached the point we're at now, where we can look each other dead in the eye and, without flinching, say how much we love each other. These days we're back to prime banter and people love listening to us for it, but there was a stage where I thought our friendship had gone forever.

For a period, a few years ago, I basically wrote him off. Every time I tried to reach out and find a time to connect, he just never got back to me. After a while, I figured I'd just ghost him right back. *So, who cares?* I told myself. Truthfully, it hurt. We've known each other since we were 15 and 16 years old, met playing Australian AFL school boys' tours, and later, briefly played at Carlton together. But when we left there – Dan retiring and me moving to Sydney to play with the Giants – it was like our friendship disappeared.

Despite being up north, I felt like I tried really hard to maintain a connection. I'd call or try and organise a catch-up, but Dan never seemed interested. So, after a while, I gave up on the guy. *Stuff it*, I thought. Obviously our mateship wasn't what I thought it was. So I stopped trying.

What I didn't know was just how much shit he was going through. Like many of us who leave a professional athletic career, Dan found himself a bit lost post-footy. When you're in the AFL, the environment is so structured, your days and life so programmed, that when it suddenly all ends, you don't know what to do with yourself. Everything you've spent your life dreaming about and working towards suddenly vanishes. Your days look very long, very empty and very scary. And Dan was really struggling.

But I had no idea. And looking back, I feel really bad about it. I didn't create the space for Dan to feel comfortable to share his worries, or even have the ability, at that stage, to know how to do that. I'd just moved to a new city, was having a last fang at footy, swimming at Coogee beach and living the dream. I literally had no clue just how much Dan was suffering.

And sure, he did a pretty good job at the time of hiding it, following the traditional model of masculinity that he, like many of us, had been modelled. Like his father, Dan bottled up his feelings and didn't talk about emotions. So there I was thinking how much of a dick he was for not returning my calls, assuming that for whatever reason he'd decided against me, that he was living his best life ignoring me . . . always imagining it was about me. And never understanding that, actually, it was about what he was going through.

Nobody, least of all me, knew that Dan was spending his nights battling with himself, alone, trying to find some purpose, a way to feel happy again. Until one night, as he explains it, he broke down and told his dad just how much he was suffering – and was completely taken by surprise when his dad replied that he too had struggled with the same dark challenges. That was a turning point for Dan, and thankfully, in the end, for our friendship. He started seeing a psych and began reaching out, and I think I've had a chance to make up for that time where I wasn't as good a friend as I should have been. These days we inspire each other, have a shitload of fun, talk deep and work hard together.

I guess what I'm saying about friendship and mates and vulnerability is that sometimes, probably most of the time, it's not about you. It's quite likely – in those moments when you're thinking your mate has blanked you – that something might be going on for them. Find a way to let them know you're there if they need you, but give them space to work things out the way that they want to. Trust that, like the seasons, time will help. That's what I'm focused on nowadays. Trying to be the best mate I can be. Fun, sure. Up for a laugh and a fair few games of golf, definitely. But most of all, there in the hard times and for the honest chats.

At the end of the day – literally at the end of my last day, at my funeral – if people remember me as a great guy who was there for his mates, I'll count that as a solid outcome. That's what I'd love to be known as, for sure. Being liked is great, but being respected – someone who's trusted and who people turn to for help – that's what's important.

Not everyone will love you – and that's a win

Despite all that, I still don't love it when people don't like me. Honestly, I struggle with that one. And I think everyone does to some extent. There are some exceptions to the rule, but I don't know anyone who leaves a party going, *Yeah, they fucking hate me. Result. Great night.*

It's something I really want to get a lot more comfortable with, but it's not easy. In footy, if people don't like you, they're not afraid to let you know about it. And I heard about it. Which, when I was part of it all, didn't bother me that much because I knew it wasn't really me they hated; just the way I played footy.

When I started the podcast, I was excited for listeners to get to know the real me. Just me and a microphone, chatting away, absolutely nothing to hide behind. And now that you know me for who I am, hopefully you enjoy hanging out with me too. It wasn't easy in the beginning, though. Being so open felt pretty raw and just a little bit terrifying. If people got to know the real me and still hated me then I'd have nowhere to hide.

So I had to learn, and it's a hard thing to deal with, but . . . there'll always be someone who doesn't like you. You can be the nicest person in the world and spend every waking minute trying to win over everyone you meet and you'll still miss a few. That's just how it is.

It's the same for everyone. Think about a role model, someone you really admire, or your favourite celebrity in the world. Could be a sports star, or a musician, or an actor, or whatever you're into. If I had to pick an example of one of mine off the top of my head I'd go with journalist and film-maker Louis Theroux. Theroux is a huge inspiration for me in the way he makes media – he's curious about people and really does the hard yards to make amazing interviews and incredible shows. He's totally fearless – gangs, Neo-Nazis, nothing seems to scare him. He's even done a film on the Church of Scientology which has a very well-known history of lawyering up and making life hard for anyone who spills dirt on them.

Celebrity-wise, there's not many people I admire more. I love, love, love Louis Theroux. But he's not for everyone. A lot of people don't like Louis Theroux. The Scientology community probably don't like Louis Theroux at all. But that doesn't affect my opinion of the guy or his work. If I were to find out that half the world hates Louis Theroux, I'm still going to love him as much as I did before I learned that.

Be like Vegemite

There's an analogy that really helps me get my head around it: Vegemite. Classic Australian breakfast icon. How do you feel about Vegemite? Maybe you don't love it. Maybe you do. If you do, you probably have strong opinions about how it goes on the toast. Just a little scrape with the edge of the knife or drown the bread in it? With butter, margarine or nothing at all? You get the idea. Your taste won't be the same as the next guy, even on something as straightforward as Vegemite toast. Then if you zoom out, you'll see that Vegemite is an Aussie thing and Australians only make up 0.3 per cent of people on the planet. So 97 per cent of the people on this planet don't know about Vegemite and would probably think it's a pretty fucking weird thing to eat for breakfast if they did. But does that change how you're going to feel about it?

That was a good thing for me to understand. It's important to know that even if a proportion of people who listen to my podcast hate me, it's not going to affect the people who do like me. Whenever I get to the stage where it's clear that someone doesn't like me, I've learned to take a sort of pride in it. Because I've come to understand that if you want to make an impact then you have to say and do things that some people are going to disagree with. You'll never have everyone in the world like what you're saying or agree with how you're saying it. That's just not how the world works.

If I tried to make a podcast that made every listener happy then it would be absolutely shithouse. I'd rather make a product that some people like, while knowing that a lot of people just aren't going to click with it. It's fine. I hope that if they don't like it they can still respect the fact that I'm doing something that's real to me and connects with the people who are into it.

Which, to bring this back around to friendship, is a good attitude to take into your relationships with mates. Surround yourself with people that you respect, as well as like, and try to make yourself someone worthy of their respect too. Be a good mate, be kind, have their back, be loyal – those qualities are more important than trying to get everyone's approval. Because you're never going to get it.

Be a good mate, be kind, have their back, be loyal – those qualities are more important than trying to get everyone's approval.

You are you, which is going to work for some people and not for others. And that's actually a great thing, because when you surround yourself with the right people, people you respect, then they are going to help you shine.

PS: While you're out there being the best mate you can be, don't forget to be a great mate to the most important person in your life: you.

CHAPTER 8

BE YOUR OWN BEST MATE

What would you do with a mate who was always putting you down? If someone you'd grown up with and known your whole life got into the habit of talking shit about you and undermining your confidence, how long would you put up with it before you told him he was being an arsehole?

Think about the last interaction you had with a mate when they were doing it tough. I don't mean a full-blown crisis necessarily, no life-or-death level stuff – not a nuclear war or an AFL grand final – but ordinary, run-of-the-mill stressful shit. Like, they didn't get the grade they wanted at school, or got sacked from their job, or dumped by their girlfriend/boyfriend. How did you talk to them? What sort of language and tone of voice did you use to try to cheer them up?

Now, recall the way you spoke to yourself the last time something went badly for you. Did you use the same kind of language? Were you anywhere near as empathetic and kind to yourself as you would be for a mate in the same situation? If you're anything like me, probably not.

I don't remember exactly where I first heard it, but one of the most important lessons I've learned is that you need to figure out how to be your own best mate. So true. If my best mate was going through something I would be straight over there delivering my famous Dylan Buckley good advice and support. 'We've all been there, mate. Don't even stress. We'll get through it. Mate, you're a legend, you will work it out.'

But as soon as it was just me talking to myself – especially during my footy career when anxiety was really tearing me a new one – trying to work out how to move forward when things were rough, I basically told myself, *Fuck you. You're a dickhead. How could you fuck this up*? And all that sort of thing. Basically, things I wouldn't say to my worst enemy and certainly not to a mate.

That's a horrible way to treat anybody, let alone yourself. How are you meant to be happy when you're constantly about to punch-on with your own self-esteem? You have to learn to be nice to yourself. You must be your own best friend and catch yourself out on those thoughts. You wouldn't tolerate someone treating your mate like that, so why bully yourself? You're a person too, and you deserve to be treated with respect. Especially by yourself.

For the longest time I used to tell myself I wasn't good enough. I'd literally be sitting there, telling myself, *I want this thing, but I'm never going to get it. I can't do it.* Before a big footy game, when I should have been getting excited and getting my mind into a dominating, athletic, goal-kicking mindset, I had little Dylan Buckley on my shoulder instead, talking shit.

You're dreaming, I'd say to myself. *You're never going to touch the ball, let alone get a kick. It's never going to happen. Forget it.*

At the time, I never gave it much thought. It was just the way I'd always talked to myself and it never seemed weird to me, until in my final days at the Giants, a psychologist at the the club flagged it with me.

'You're really hard on yourself,' he said. 'Try and catch yourself out with your language.'

Basically, he wanted me to take notice when I was thinking negatively and to flip it. Take the same initial thought, but express it in a more positive way. Instead of saying, 'I *can't* do this,' when I was up against an obstacle I couldn't see a way around, I should say, 'I haven't done this *yet*.'

It sounds simple, but it was so powerful. Once I started changing my internal language, things really started to turn around. It became addictive. When I became aware of how much I'd been sabotaging myself in my own head I was pretty taken aback. I realised it was no fucking wonder that things weren't working out for me, with me constantly telling myself that things weren't going to.

Instead of putting myself down when I'd had a shit game, for example, I started telling myself not to let it get me down. *Don't stress, Dyl. Don't worry about it. You're working hard, I know things haven't gone your way today, but you're a decent guy and it's going to work out for you.*

It was crazy what a difference it made. Once I started telling myself I was a good guy and getting better at it and doing it more often, I eventually started to believe it. Which meant the world started to believe it. It was a big power move in terms of how I operated. My tolerance for being unkind to myself absolutely disappeared.

You start to forgive yourself a little bit for making mistakes and to see your challenges more realistically. It gives you a bit more perspective because it effectively takes you out of your own body and helps you talk through your problems in a healthy way – the way you would with a mate – with compassion, empathy and logic. *Alright, well, we stuffed up here. Could it have gone better? Yeah, we definitely could have done better. But let's learn from it. And the next time we'll do better. Let's not get upset unless we make that same mistake again.*

When I first made the decision to go easy on myself and start trying to flip my natural tendency to beat myself up into something more positive, my footy career was ending. So the discrepancy between the way I was asking myself to think and the reality of the situation could not have been larger. Externally, a lot of people in my life (and total strangers online) looked at my sacking as a bad thing. You know,

'Poor Dyl, he's gone and done it again. Now he's sacked, he's got nothing, what's he going to do?'

Internally, though, I was running with a different narrative. *How good is this going to be?* I said to myself. *This is so exciting. Footy is done, but not many people get eight years in footy, living the dream. Now you've done that, and you've got so many cool connections out of it. Now you're free to build yourself this platform to be able to do what you want to do. You get to move back to Melbourne and be around your friends and family. How exciting is that? Your life is a blank canvas. You can do anything. This is unbelievable.*

I didn't even necessarily believe a lot of the things I was saying. It might not have been how I truly felt at that moment. But I knew, psychologically, that was where I wanted to get to. I wanted to feel good about it. So I told myself and the world that I did, until one day I actually did feel that way.

It wasn't easy at first. Giving up exaggerated negativity and self-deprecation as a defence mechanism was difficult. When things went wrong, the reflex was to make it into a joke, like, 'Fuck my life'. But self-deprecation and sarcasm are not great. While it can be funny, it's not humour, strictly speaking. It's hostility. It's the passive-aggressive way to make yourself understood when you're not being honest about what you really want to say. That applies even – maybe especially – to self-talk. As comedian Hannah Gadsby points out in her special *Nanette*, 'Self-deprecation isn't humility, it's humiliation. We put ourselves down in order to be given permission to speak.'[9]

I once heard that when you're talking negatively about yourself, your brain and body respond as though you really mean what you're saying. I don't even know if it's scientifically true, but I've found it's true for me. Where the mind goes, the body tends to follow. When I say out loud, 'This is shit. This situation is making me miserable,' then it becomes true. So, I'm very careful with what I vocalise. I don't put negativity into the world because I know it'll bounce back on me and become real. Even during a really hard time, I'll never, never say anything negative out loud to myself. Because that moment when you're struggling is when you most need a good friend, and the closest friend is always yourself. It's very hard to silence those negative voices in your head, but you have a choice to not give them a voice in the real world.

Words create worlds

Hunter Johnson is the CEO of Man Cave, an emotional-intelligence charity that has impacted the lives of over 50,000 young men and advocates for a better kind of masculinity. He's also a regular star of my podcast and, over time, has become a good mate.[10]

'Words create worlds,' Hunter tells me. 'That's the power of the stories we tell ourselves. The stories we tell ourselves, or that we want to believe, become true. Because they shape our inner world, which then shapes our behaviours, shapes our attitudes, and shapes what we choose to do.'

Hunter speaks from experience. He had to rebuild himself when, at 16, he sustained a rugby injury so brutal it nearly killed him. His shattered leg required six operations, two blood transfusions and two skin grafts. The wounds were mental, too. His identity – built around being a strong, stoic gun on the rugby field – was shattered along with his leg. It was the start of a journey where he got to know another side of himself. As he tells it, the injury gave him a chance to press the refresh button on his identity and see how he was showing up for his mates, his family and himself. That started a journey to explore the self, leadership and emotional intelligence, which in turn would see him become a leader of rethinking the stories boys and men tell themselves about who they are.

Part of Hunter rediscovering his identity was coming to the understanding that in traditional Australian masculinity, men aren't equipped with the language to be kind and empathetic to each other, or themselves. 'I saw a lot of guys – including myself – feeling trapped by it, but they never really had the space, or the language, or the permission, to talk about some of the challenges that we were dealing with as teenage boys,' he says. 'Language is how we make sense of the world . . . That's why the way that we talk to ourselves is actually significant.'

Being able to understand and articulate how you're feeling is a real issue for boys in our culture because we're not trained in how to do it. In fact, we're often encouraged *not* to. We're not paying attention to how we talk to ourselves and it's so easy to fail to notice when we're being unkind to ourselves. For example, when I was younger and someone on the footy field would give me a bit of a spray when I fumbled a ball, my 'bloke persona' would encourage me to stand up for myself. But if I were to look in the mirror and tell myself, 'You dickhead, you really cooked it out there today,' I'd have nobody to stand up for me but myself.

That's where positive self-talk comes in. And it's something that really takes practice. As I'm writing this book I've realised how, recently, I've fallen back into the trap of not being a very good friend to myself. Because things are pretty good for me right now, I've stopped being proactive about maintaining my mental health, which is one of the most important ways you can be your own best mate.

Proactive versus reactive mental health

What we could be better at, according to Dr Zac Seidler, is treating our mental health as well as we do our bodies. As a clinical psychologist, a Senior Research Fellow at Melbourne Uni and Director of Mental Health Training at Movember, Zac is considered a leading men's mental health expert and an incredibly eloquent speaker on the subject. He spoke to me on the pod.[11]

'We need to be proactive, not reactive,' says Zac. 'There's too much crisis. That's the whole men's mental health game.'

It's safe to say that Aussies – Aussie men in particular – suffer from trying to be too tough, too staunch and too stoic. It's a cliché because it's too bloody true, that an Aussie guy won't go to the doctor unless he has to limp there. Some really hard nuts, footy players of my dad's generation, would literally have rather run around on broken bones than take themselves out of the game.

Thankfully the modern era is more progressive about looking after health. These days, when you're injured you do rehab and recovery so that the injury doesn't become a crisis. That's also why we watch what we eat, exercise and actively monitor our physical strengths and weaknesses: to make ourselves fit and, if you're into that sort of thing, achieve a nice, respectable rig. In general, we're good at that.

When mental health stuff starts to pop up, however – feeling sad, or anxious, feelings of depression, or maybe drinking or partying too hard – our culture still tells men to ignore it; tough it out and hope it just goes away. We don't actually go and get help until we hit a crisis point. Which is exactly the wrong thing to do, believe me. I tried to manage my anxiety on my own and endured a slow-rolling crisis for eight years of game nights.

Being proactive with your mental health is about seeking help and resources and being kind to yourself *before* you get to the stage where something really bad is happening. For each person those actions will look different. Personally, when I'm starting to get a bit anxious or overwhelmed by life, I've learned to listen to the early warning bells. I realise, *Fuck, I need to do something to relax this buzz, now.* Whether it's to go for a run, or get out and see some friends, or get off the drink for a bit – those are things that work for me, depending on the situation.

Dr Zac incorporates several options. He swims every day, he meditates, but an essential part of his proactive mental health is connecting with his mates. 'I've got my [physical] things, but sometimes I need people – I need someone to hold me.'

Work out your rituals and make them work for you

Man Cave's Hunter Johnson has his own mental health rituals and routines too. He lists checking in with mates as one of his most important tools. For more than four years he's never missed his weekly phone call with his best friend, regardless of where they are in the world. It's something they stick to, even if one of them doesn't feel up to it, because the commitment matters and the communication is vital.

'I love being around people,' says Hunter. 'I'm a big sharer. So if something bad happens to me, I'm like, *I gotta tell people.* So I create rhythms in my life of checking in with people and having non-negotiable things built into my week, my days, my months.'

Hunter's advice is to take the time to slow down and listen to what your gut is telling you about what you need. That could mean going for a run, or journaling, or meditation, or cooking something. Whatever it is that helps you start sorting through all the shit that's ticking away at the back of your mind before it reaches critical mass. We all have to deal with things that are going to tax our mental health – but it makes a massive difference if you can deal with them as they come up, rather than wait for a crisis point.

'My language for it is, are you playing offence? Or are you playing defence?'

Hunter likes to set proactive mental health habits using the gaming framework because that suits his psychology. 'I think for many guys our mindset is very competitive and very conquest driven. So, if that's my nature, let's just apply that to my wellbeing.'

Using that analogy, neglecting yourself is a defensive game. If your mental health is a basketball court where the opposition is getting regular slam-dunks, that's not ideal. On the other hand, if you're on the offensive and putting little things in place to keep the ball up the court near your own basket, then your game will be better all over.

For me, I've got all these little things that add up to a good offensive game. There are the big ones, like going to see my psychologist. Then there's everyday ones, like my diet. I don't eat meat, partially for ethical reasons, but more because I just don't like it. I realised that every time I ate meat I felt crook afterwards, so I cut it out and felt fantastic. I've also got lots of little, really weird ones, like drinking water as a calming method. I've always drunk a lot of water and somewhere along the line I realised that when I'm really stressed, if I drink a litre of water, it calms me down.

It goes back all the way to when I was in school. One time I got sent to the principal's office. While I was waiting to go in and talk to her, I was pretty emotional, the anxiety just kept cranking up and up. Seeing how uptight I was, the receptionist offered me a cup of water, then another, then another. By the time I went in to see the principal, I'd had six cups and felt weirdly calm. Something about the act of chugging all that water had settled me. I was able to go in and have a good, reasonable conversation, instead of being over-emotional.

Fuck knows how that works, but it does. I think it's a very specific form of meditation. Maybe specific only to me. So find out what works for you and add it to your proactive mental health toolkit.

Swim versus sink

According to Dr Zac, proactivity in mental health is about taking the time to regularly check in. He compares it to being out on the ocean. The proactive approach is to realise that your boat is leaking and start bailing it out as you head back for shore, whereas the reactive approach is, 'I'll wait until I'm sinking and then I'll start to swim.'

He says a good way to get on top of stuff early is by asking yourself, 'What are my intentions here? What am I striving for? And who is this person that I am moving towards? What am I becoming and how can I do this a little differently?' It's not that proactive mental health means staying constantly on the alert for things that stress us out, or trying to live like saints. It's okay to have fun. It's okay to have a pizza and a couple of cordials on the weekend.

Actually, that's considered best practice if connecting with your mates over a beer is what helps you deal with everyday stresses. Zac says it's important for young men to have fun. That there's room to do things that aren't necessarily 'helpful' for you all the time, but just to keep the long term in mind. There's a way to proactively allow yourself to work out where you're at *and* where you want to be, which is a far better gameplay than the alternative.

During one of our chats, Zac loosely translated this quote from French philosopher, Albert Camus. 'In the midst of winter, I discovered in me an invincible summer.'[12] Beach-loving Zac loves this one, especially in Melbourne where it's been known to hail in the middle of summer. It reflects the notion that what's happening inside your head isn't necessarily what's happening in the outside world. You can make decisions 'that can reshape the way that you're perceiving your own reality,' Zac explains. 'Surround yourself with the right people, do the right things. You can create happiness for yourself in many ways.'

Let's come back to the idea of thinking of the man in the mirror as your best mate. If you saw your best mate stressed out, or eating shit food night after night, or getting so drunk he's pissed himself, then you'd be worried about him. You'd ask him what was wrong and what you could do to help. Now it's time to take that one step further and treat yourself the same way.

'I think that the reason those check-ins are so difficult for lots of guys is because it's a [new] language,' says Zac. 'It's a language and a skill and a muscle, whatever you wanna call it, that takes time to get used to.'

Changing our language is one of the easiest ways we can be kind to each other. And when it comes to being kind to yourself, the language of self-talk is everything.

Friendship Toolkit

- Being liked is not the same thing as being respected. It's okay to want both, but knowing the difference is important. Respect means people know they can rely on you in an emergency.
- Be like Vegemite. Most of the world doesn't like Vegemite, but if you know, you know – there's nothing better. Vegemite doesn't change to get the whole world to like it. It just keeps being awesome for those who appreciate it.
- Be a good mate to your friends. Be kind, loyal, generous – those qualities are more important than trying to get everyone's approval.
- Be a good mate to yourself. If a mate were going through a hard time, how would you support them? Next time you're struggling, try talking to yourself like you would a mate – you'll be kinder to yourself and it'll help you think things through more realistically.
- When it comes to being kind to yourself, language is everything. The stories we tell ourselves about ourselves help shape how we feel. 'Words create worlds'.
- There's too much crisis in men's mental health. Looking after your mental health is so much better than reacting to crisis. Don't wait until you're drowning to learn to swim.

MINDSET

CHAPTER 9
IN THE EYE OF THE HURRICANE

Let's talk about mindset. For me, mindset is one of life's fundamentals. Something I wish I'd gotten a better grip on earlier. Basically, your mindset is the collection of beliefs you have about yourself. The stories you tell yourself about yourself, like, *I'm a gun footy player*, or *I'm shit at maths*. These beliefs – good and bad – collectively add up to create your understanding of your place in the world. As such, they determine your behaviour, outlook and mental attitude.

The problem is, unless you're regularly in the practice of being your own best mate, then the stories you're telling yourself about who you are probably aren't very kind. For many, they can be unkind and untrue. That's worth paying attention to. Because it's hard to succeed in life, in anything, if your mindset is undercutting you. Nothing in your life – talents, goals, desires, relationships – is easy if your mindset is working against you.

It's hard to succeed in life, in anything, if your mindset is undercutting you.

I'm wary of anyone who says they know what the most important thing in the world is, but let me tell you this: mindset is so important. When I found ways to manage my mindset it flipped the script on my whole existence. Certain techniques and tools, which I'll go into next, helped me manage my mental health. So that when anxiety was really kicking me in the arse, I had ways to short-circuit it.

I've spoken to a lot of legends over the years – high achievers in sport or business or generally in life. They come from hugely different worlds, different backgrounds, but collectively, the one thing that really stands out to me is their mindset.

High-performance coach Emma Murray is an expert in how to get the best from yourself which is why she's a regular on the pod.[13] You'd have to go pretty far to find someone better. In sports circles she's a bit of a secret weapon. Emma works with athletes to build powerful mindsets grounded in the psychology and practice of mindfulness, which she calls 'high-performance mindfulness'. She says that mindfulness, in a nutshell, is all about staying present and not attaching to the outcome and allowing yourself to relax or de-stress in that moment, which allows you to think clearly and move accordingly. Having trained up in and taught this for decades, in 2016 Emma experienced a personal tragedy that put all her career-skills training to the test.

Early that year, on an ordinary, sunny summer's day, Emma's eldest son, Will, a few weeks shy of his 14th birthday, went to the beach with a group of friends. He jumped off the pier and suffered a spinal cord injury that left him a quadriplegic, with no feeling or movement from the chest or shoulders down.

'That moment throws your entire family into a hurricane. It's something you cannot even put words around . . . I remember this moment very clearly where I was taken into a little room with a doctor and a psychologist, and they said to me, "Emma, the grief of spinal cord injury is worse than death. Because the reality of a spinal cord injury is that it takes work. So much work. An unbelievable amount of work."'

The doctors told Emma that Will's injury was permanent and would cost close to a million dollars to manage over his lifetime. For Will to live with the injury, the family home would have to be renovated to allow for ramps, specialist equipment would need to be purchased, and carers would need to be employed. Most people who acquire a spinal cord injury are in hospital for more than a year after first being admitted because their life on the outside needs a complete overhaul. Emma felt overwhelmed as she took all this in and knew she had to find a way to deal with the situation.

'It was in that moment that I really, really remember thinking, *I need to bring my best to this moment. I need to stand up, I need to take action*,' she recalls. 'At that point, action meant holding onto mindfulness. It was a lifeline.'

She remembers one long night, when Will was in a coma in ICU, just walking up and down the hospital hallway over and over again, doing walking mindfulness meditation. She couldn't be still or find her breath in sitting meditation, and so, to anchor herself, she walked, concentrating intensely on feeling her feet, hips and shoulders in motion.

'The second I wasn't in that state of hardcore mindfulness I would just go to the most horrific places,' she says. 'All of a sudden we needed a house renovated, we needed carers, we needed to get Will out of hospital. Mindfulness got me up, it kept me standing.'

The situation Emma's family faced was horrific, but she's grateful she had her meditation practice, developed over years of research, to ground her. It's part of why she continues to bring meditation and mindfulness into sporting clubs and businesses – environments that are typically too alpha-blokey and rough-headed for their own good.

Often when a high-performance team hears they are going to implement a mindfulness program, they aren't interested, says Emma. 'They're like, "Oh, I don't need that, I don't want that." But when survival requires it, you grip onto it differently. So I tell them, "Life is rugged for all of us. It is truly rugged and recent years have taken that ruggedness to another level."

'But for most of us, we're hanging out in this storm. We go out each day, we get wet, we get drenched, we are pretty miserable. It's grey, it's cold. We come home, we wake up, we do it again the next day and we do it over and over again.

'For some of us, we have a moment where that storm gets instantly upgraded to a hurricane. For us, that was Will's spinal cord injury. All of a sudden, when your storm becomes a hurricane, you can't do it day in, day out. You just can't keep getting beaten around the head. Your survival requires you to get to the centre of the hurricane, which is that stillness. Because in that centre of the hurricane, there is no wind, there is no storm.'

'Just relax' is some reliably bad advice

Emma understands the weight of pressure at an elite performance level because she's been there. In her teens she played netball at a national level and attended the AIS, but her career was dogged by one injury after another. It got to the point where she found herself in a state of shame because she couldn't crack two games in a row.

'Athletes get told to relax a lot,' says Emma, 'So I tell them, "Stop worrying about other people, don't worry about losing. Just relax when you kick for goal in front of 100 thousand people." We get told *what* to do, but we don't often get told *how* to do it.'

From netball, Emma went into coaching, where she became fascinated by trying to solve why her athletes would follow one really great day with a terrible day. What, she wanted to know, was helping or hindering them to tap into their best?

'When I started working with athletes, I was always really confused about how you could get into that state of relaxation when you're driving a car at 300 kilometres an hour, or you're in the middle of the MCG,' says Emma. 'And I didn't even know if that was the right state to be in.'

Emma began her journey with meditation around the age of 20. After meditation, she went on to study a lot of other mind-management techniques and traditions and slowly began incorporating her learnings into her work with athletes. Over time it became increasingly clear that meditation and mindfulness practices were invaluable for high-performance athletes.

Eye of the tiger

Every athlete I've met who's worked with Emma speaks so highly of her work and what her coaching has helped them achieve. Not just in sports, but holistically in their life. One of the best testaments to the impact of her work is the success of the Richmond AFL club.

It's fair to say that Richmond was struggling in 2016. They hadn't won a premiership in 37 years and had suffered a shattering 100-point defeat to Sydney in the elimination final. The public were calling for a complete rebuild of the team – sack the board, the coach, the captain, and start again. Richmond needed something to shake the mental pressure of their losing streak and hoped that Emma's coaching would be the silver bullet they needed.

Emma's approach was to figure out how to get more players to bring their A game more often; to switch from the B to the A game quicker and stay there longer. She reckoned that's where Richmond would find its performance gains.

'The first thing I say to an athlete is that you can't *lose* your skill. It doesn't go missing. It doesn't disappear midway through a game. So, we have to recognise that we've gone into that stress response – which is not designed to make us good at football or good at our jobs, but to keep us alive.

'To fix this, you don't have to get fitter, or stronger, or do more practice. Most of these athletes are doing the work. They are as fit as each other, as strong as each other. They've got their skills in place. Now we just have to teach them how to get into the right state quicker and stay there longer.'

The mindset that Emma helps athletes build enables them to perform even under the incredible strains of pro-level performance. Elite sport comes with a weight of expectation, media scrutiny, no private life, and criticism from left, right and centre. All while trying to kick the bloody ball through the goal posts.

Emma's guidance turned out to be a champion intervention for Richmond which has gone on to have a ripple effect through the whole league. It took them from 13th on the ladder to a premiership in *one year*. Of course, her influence wasn't the only factor that turned Richmond's fortunes around so spectacularly, but ever since, mindfulness and mindset have become integral to pretty much every club's game plan.

A game versus B game

Emma regularly talks about our A game and our B game. Our A game is when we're firing on all cylinders, feel calm and have the clarity of thought to use our physical and mental talents and training as we know we can. Our B game is when our state of mind prevents us from bringing our best to a situation – like when I used to run out on the field and the anxiety would absolutely cook me.

In training, when the stakes were low and I was having a great time with my mates, I could bring my A game. But under those lights at the MCG, out came the anxiety. The ironic part is that, of course, it was the worry that I wouldn't perform that fucked my ability to perform. That's what gave me my B game. So why would my brain do me dirty like that?

Human beings evolved in dangerous environments, Emma explains, where the ability to recognise and react to threats was necessary for survival. That wiring is still part of us. She gives the example of a caveman who runs into a tiger. Faced with death, the caveman's brain creates a stress response – a massive fight-or-flight adrenaline rush that helps him deal with the situation. While the stress response is in play he's hyper-focused, all his attention on the threat right in front of him.

'The caveman would either kill that tiger, get away from that tiger, or the tiger would kill him. But the fight would end some way,' explains Emma. After the fight, the surviving caveman goes back to his cave where he rests, recovers, his physical alarm fades and his mental focus returns.

The problem is, we're still operating with caveman brains in today's world. We have less intense stressors than a tiger, but way, way more of them. And our brains aren't so good at telling one threat from another. A car cutting you off in traffic, or your boss yelling at you, or a social media post that really pisses you off for reasons you can't quite put your finger on, all affect us the same way the tiger made the caveman shit his pants.

They aren't life-changing traumas, but they are stressful. And they all add up. Each feels like a tiny little fight with a tiger. We fight tigers all day. At work, tigers. Watching *Shawshank Redemption*, tigers. At night in bed scrolling through our phones, tigers. Our brains are perceiving tigers all around.

While our brains are still very good at reacting to these 'tigers', they're not so good at calming down afterwards. Emma calls each of these situations minor stressors. And they build up. To the point where, when an actual problem comes along, you're already full-peaking, so then you get completely overwhelmed. 'By now these minor stressors feel like a big stress and we've lost the ability to break that stress cycle.'

And that's a problem. Because the stress cycle never ends on its own. We have to deliberately put in place things to break it.

'If I could give one piece of information to everyone, it's that anxiety is a survival wiring,' Emma tells me. 'It's not because you're weak, it's not because you have a mental illness. It's not because you are struggling. Your mind is wired to go there. And once we actually know that, then we can learn how to catch it.'

Emma says that once she's identified that she's having a stress response she can put one of her mental levers into action. 'It's not about telling you to suck it up and not worry about it. It's actually knowing, *Well yes, it's normal to be in this state, but how do I shift it? What tools do I have that can pull me out of this? Well, I can go to my breath.'*

Emma's practice involves recognising that you're having a stress response, knowing it's normal and also knowing how to shift out of it. That means using tools to help redirect that stress response to bring us from our B game back to our A game. 'You're still gonna have those B game moments. But if you've got those levers, you can snap out of it quicker.'

Emma breaks mindfulness down into a three-part process:

1. Build your awareness.
2. Get your shit together.
3. Step into your best.

For the Richmond Tigers, that meant teaching them tricks from the world of meditation. If they were sceptical at first, they were converted when they saw the turnaround in their champion players once they got out of their heads and into an A game mindset.

Meditation is taking the rubbish out (of your mind)

'Once we have more awareness [of our stress response], then we want to start to regulate our emotions,' Emma says. 'And to do that, we need a way to clean out all that stuff in our mind, clear it out, reset ourselves. And this is where the meditation, or the mindfulness, comes into place. Meditation is taking the rubbish out of your mind.'

I was first introduced to mindset and meditation at Carlton. I hated it. Was absolutely rubbish at it. The way I learned it was just way too full-on. I was assigned two 20-minute meditations a day, which is hard even for Zen masters. My mind and body just absolutely could not sit still for that long.

I knew that I was stressed out, but concentrating on that fact only made it worse. Turns out, I'm not alone. Emma has observed that people in high pressure, high expectation environments like professional athletes, sometimes find meditation a stretch too far. 'Some people find sitting down and meditating too hard. We're in this hypervigilant state and that can stress us even more. So, they're like, *What the hell do I do with this?*'

That's what happened to me. I tried meditating for three days and abandoned it completely. I just said no. I couldn't do it anymore, it was too much. Like so many things we're talking about here, ultimately, it's finding out what works best for you. As Emma reminds me, there's no one right way to do mindfulness.

For some people, full-on lotus pose, transcendental meditation is the thing. For others, it might be as basic as taking time to watch the rain. Literally. Emma sometimes has footy teams she's working with stand at the window and watch the rain fall to calm their minds and practise mindfulness. 'Concentrating on a cloud can be meditation. There's one where you just stare at your hand and follow the lines on your palm and it drops you into a meditative state. Meditation is just giving your attention a job.'

Obviously one that's not available to me all the time, but other tools are. One that clicks really well for me is 'breath work'.

And breathe

Breath is one of the simplest and, for me, best mindfulness tools out there. If you can concentrate on your breath, it brings you back to the body and changes the message going up to your mind. The simple act of concentrating on your breath is calming. It reminds the body that it's not in danger and from there it's easier to drop into acceptance of the present. Yes, you might be in a shit situation, but now that you're here and you're not actually in danger, how can you bring your best to this moment?

Over time I've gotten better and better at dropping into my breath when I feel anxious. Because the brain is like a muscle: if you train it in specific techniques and practices it'll get stronger along the way.

There are heaps of simple breath meditations, but one that works for me is the '3, 4, 5'. It couldn't be easier. You breathe in for three seconds, hold for four seconds, then breathe out for five seconds. Just the act of making your exhale longer than your inhale trips the mechanism that's telling you to panic and helps calm you down.

It's the kind of meditation trick that will work even when you're in the middle of the MCG with a massive ruckman about to flatten you into the mud.

Practising mindfulness techniques can help regulate your adrenaline levels when you feel stressed, and the more you practise, the better your ability to cope with stress will get.

Practising mindfulness techniques can help regulate your adrenaline levels when you feel stressed, and the more you practise, the better your ability to cope with stress will get. Research suggests that mindfulness practice changes the brain. Scientists are working on proving it, but one 2018 Harvard study showed promise. After eight weeks of mindfulness practice, meditators showed an increase in grey brain matter detectable by MRI.[14]

But not everyone has an MRI machine lying around. Sometimes those mental gains aren't as easily measured as the physical ones. I can go to the gym and get bigger and you'll see results almost straight away. You can look in the mirror at the end of a season and go, 'Yep, that's a high-performance rig.' But with mindset it's harder to see.

It's important to remember that mindfulness is not a one-time thing. If you want to move closer to a high-performance mindset, it's about making and implementing regular tiny habits which get you incrementally better at managing your focus and emotions. All the while knowing you'll never get it perfect because there's no such thing.

Nobody brings their A game to every situation, or every day. I think back to the best games of footy I ever played. Even when I was dominating out there, I couldn't bring my best every minute. I moved between my A and B games the entire 80 minutes, even if I wasn't aware of what I was doing, or why. Nobody can sustain an elite level of performance mindset at all times. We'd overload.

Even with what I do now, as the very happy and grateful host of a podcast, my results vary. When I record a pod, that's me absolutely putting my A game forward. I'm trying to be as perfect as I can possibly be because I want to make the best pod I can for the listener. But that's one hour of the week I'm on my A game. Everything behind the scenes is much more B game. The amount of shit I stuff up is something I'm very aware of and try and be open about. Because in sport and business, people tend only to show you their wins.

Sport is the worst because it's a sort of de facto religion in this country. When our sports heroes are shown to be imperfect, it comes as this big shock to people. The public seem to act so surprised. But nobody is perfect. Obviously I'm not. And I'm happy not to be. But I'm always working to bring my A game a little closer and spend a little less time in the Bs. Practising mindfulness is part of that.

Be like a leaf in the wind

Finding that mindset is all about finding equilibrium. For most of my life, until I took steps to actively manage my emotional state, I was either way too high or way too low. When things were good, I felt unstoppable, everything was the best it could be and I was ready for anything. But when things were bad, I was completely unable to deal with it. Something would knock me down and suddenly I would be having the shittiest day ever.

Equilibrium is learning to keep yourself anchored in the middle, knowing that your emotional state is like a wave – you go up, but then you are able come down and to centre yourself. You have a win and you have the presence of mind to know you've done a great job, congratulate yourself, celebrate it and then get back to work. The same goes if you get knocked down – give it a minute and you'll rise back up again. Take the time you need when you have a really shit experience, but tell yourself, *You know what, it isn't that bad, let's move on to the next thing and come back up.* When you're really in a good, resilient mindset, you feel like you can react to anything – go with the flow like a leaf in the wind.

It helps remembering that emotions are temporary things. You might be having the shittiest day on record, but ride it out, it'll break and a new wave will come along soon enough. I've learned to stay in the middle and enjoy the ride. You can get dunked pretty bloody hard, but sooner or later you'll pop back up and remember to breathe.

One of the biggest lessons I've learned about myself is around emotional decision making. I'm quite an emotional person – that's not exactly a secret. When things happen to me, I'm pretty quick to feel something about it and I'm a bit of an open book when it comes to my emotions. I don't gamble, which is good, because I'd be a shithouse poker player. I get excited and react to things way too easily. Because of that, I've stuffed up a lot of things, just from reacting on emotion. Whether it's work, or footy, or relationships with other people, I've made important decisions in the heat of the moment when I shouldn't have. We don't always make good choices when we're reacting with our emotions.

Luckily, over time, I've worked out that my emotions are a temporary state. My emotions aren't who I am. They are just how I'm feeling in the moment. So, when something happens that makes me angry, sad, anxious, or whatever the emotion is, then I know it's probably not the best time to be making decisions that will have lasting consequences. Often, if you just give the thing 24 hours, let your immediate emotions subside, you'll come to your senses and work out what the best decision is. State of mind is temporary, but actions tend to have lasting results. I've found that those results tend to be better when I've taken time to manage my mindset, calm down a bit and return to equilibrium.

CHAPTER 10
SOME NOTES ON BEING A LEGEND

One of my favourite things about podcasting is that I never stop meeting amazing people. My job is to sit down and chat and hear the most amazing stories, learn the most inspiring stuff, hear how people achieve incredible things. While every story is different, as I've said before, the common factor among high achievers is their mindset. It's something that ultra-marathon runner and ultra-mindset expert Samantha Gash knows all about and came on the pod to share.[15]

Sam's particular speciality is what she calls a 'growth mindset' – having the courage to examine your own beliefs about yourself, try new things, and set your goals with an open mind. When she came on the pod, Sam spoke about being a very goal-oriented person and her track record speaks for itself. Sam is one of the highest achieving long-distance runners in the world. In 2010 she took on the 4 Deserts Grand Slam, running four 250-kilometre ultra-marathons – across the Atacama Crossing in Chile, Gobi March in China, Sahara Race in Egypt, and The Last Desert in Antarctica – carrying everything she needed to survive in a backpack. In doing so she made history, becoming the first woman and youngest person to have completed all four races of the Grand Slam in a calendar year.

Since then, she's been the subject of films, been a contestant on *Survivor* (where she met her future husband, props for solid multi-tasking), and become an advocate for social change. Along the way she's raised north of a million bucks for charity. So, safe to say, the woman knows how to achieve extraordinary things and the mindset it takes to do it.

'I like to say that it's 90 per cent mental, and the other ten per cent is all in your head,' Sam says. 'The mind and the body are inextricably linked, and where one goes, the other will typically follow.'

When I ask her about mindset, she describes it as that thing that fuels you to prepare yourself in every domain. The work that you put in place to be able to achieve the actual goal. It's the hard work behind the adventures and achievements, which involves sacrifice and compromise. Yes, Sam has run 1600 kilometres across the Great Himalaya Trail, but she didn't just wake up and do it one day. She had to wear out a lot of training shoes on the way.

'The real, real stuff is everything beforehand, it's the prep ticket,' she says. 'It's what you learn along the way, how you feel and who you meet and where you could go from that point.'

The high-resilience, high-growth, ultra-mindset is not something that Sam was born with. According to Sam, she learned to fix very rigid, very realistic (albeit high-difficulty) goals early in life.

'We learn early on to tell ourselves stories about ourselves. What we are good at and what we are (or are not) capable of,' she explains. 'As a child, I was very, very small and terrible in the sporting arena.'

In the field of ultra-marathons, Sam is now considered a giant. Though not in the traditional sense, maybe, because she stands at just under 152 centimetres, with a small but incredibly strong frame. She vividly remembers the schoolyard pick, when the teacher would elect two captains to select their team from classmates. I used to love the pick because I was a gun at sport and always either captain or picked first, but for Sam it was a different story. She remembers it as a horrible experience.

'I'd be the kid on the line thinking, *Please don't be one of the last two kids, you don't want to be one of the last two kids*. And invariably, I was one of the last two kids.'

If she happened to be the very last and the class was an odd number, the teacher would tell her to pick which team she wanted to be on, which was even worse, because by then she'd decided she didn't belong in either group. It was a formative experience for her; the shame of being left out. Even though she was very young, she formed the belief that success in other fields could prevent her being left behind in the future. 'Up into my mid-20s I was fearful of not being seen as successful and not being picked for the team. That sense of belonging means so much. So much of our narrative about what we're capable of stems from the stories we tell ourselves in childhood, and they can reveal themselves in a really negative way in adulthood.'

The stories we tell ourselves are powerful

As a result of those stories Sam told herself, she had little tolerance for uncertainty. This made her ambitious and driven to achieve big goals. Later in life, she realised that all the goals she set for herself had something in common: a clear path to success. If the goal was murkier – either its outcome or the path to achieving it was not clear – she set her sights on something else. Uncertainty was not an option.

As a kid Sam dreamed of being an actress on *Home and Away*, or a lawyer for the United Nations, but in the end didn't pursue either because they had no obvious paths to get there. Instead she made a more practical choice – becoming a lawyer for international law firm Baker McKenzie, with the path to high status and high income laid out in clear steps. The first of these was enrolling in a double degree in law and the performing arts at Monash University. And it was there in an acting class that a chance meeting with Aussie actor Charles 'Bud' Tingwell changed her life.

Bud gave Sam one simple piece of advice. 'His secret to success,' says Sam. 'Although he was too humble to put it that way.' Bud told her his whole life was guided by a sort of mantra: 'Just say yes. Yes to experiences. Yes to unexpected forks in the road. Yes to uncertainty and the possibility of failure.'

Just say yes. Yes to experiences. Yes to unexpected forks in the road. Yes to uncertainty and the possibility of failure.

For Sam, it was one of those life-changing brushes with another person that really sticks with you. 'You realise they're living their life in a way you aren't, but would like to be.'

At home that night, she asked herself how often she said yes? *Only when there would be a clear outcome*, she realised. If she could see a straight line from where she was at that moment to the result she wanted, then she said yes. But if yes meant taking a more ambiguous path, or going down too many pathways, or opening doors to situations and outcomes she couldn't predict, then her answer was always the same: no.

'The funny thing is, the more you say no, the less unknown paths you explore and the less doors are open to you,' Sam says. She realised that unless she changed her attitude, the doors to opportunity would remain closed. Not because they weren't available to her, but because she wouldn't see them in the first place.

Ironically, Sam realised, her anxiety towards failure, which meant taking the 'safe option' so she wouldn't 'miss out on opportunities', actually meant that doors were slamming shut all around her. In that moment it became clear just how much potential she was missing out on. So, Sam started saying yes. She tried new things and embraced them hard. Like her hippy phase where she slept in a van with other kaftan-lovers on a commune-style bus in America. She got cornrows, listened to Bob Marley and read Kerouac's *On the Road*.

For Sam, running became the biggest of her new opportunities. Not long after taking up the sport she ran her first marathon in 2008. Ten kilometres from the finish line, she 'hit the wall'. Despite her fatigue, she stumbled through the end of the race with the help of a friend, and in doing so, realised that the stories she'd told herself about her body were untrue. Through pushing herself to the limit, Sam realised the incredible strength, resilience and endurance she possessed.

'I always told myself, *I'm so small, I'm physically weak*. Which is definitely how I saw myself,' she says. But finishing that first race changed everything. From then, Sam recast herself as capable. The more things she tried, the more things she said yes to, the more opportunities arrived. She signed up to do the world's toughest races. Was a contestant on *Survivor*. Raised small fortunes for several charities across the world. All of which started because she saw the wisdom in Bud Tingwell's mantra.

'That doesn't mean that you should live your life by the successful tools of other people,' Sam says. 'But it's definitely something to consider.'

In saying yes and banishing her worries about failure, Sam unlocked the doors to success. When I finally started making media without worrying about my future in it, I found the same thing. *The important thing is the journey, not the destination.*

I've found that once you make yourself open to them, possibilities are everywhere. Yes, sometimes opportunity is given to you by other people, but most of the time, even *that* is because of something you've done. I don't mean it's a manifestation of something you've put into the world, necessarily. It could be as simple as having had a conversation, or putting yourself in a new space, or meeting new people, or thinking about something differently. Once you start saying yes, then the lines between who opens doors for you and the doors you've opened yourself start to blur.

If your mindset is one that grows and adapts, it will better serve you as you discover more about yourself. If you make saying yes a habit, then the universe will start saying yes back. The right mindset has a way of manifesting – I don't mean in a magical, woo-woo sort of way, but in a real-world sense. When you meet someone standing in a door you want to go through, they realise, *Oh, this bloke's having a crack, he's got drive, let's give him a go.*

That all starts with mindset.

No expectations, no limits

Even before I first met Sam and heard her articulate the idea much better than I ever could, I'd been saying yes. For me, the first half of my podcasting career was a big sliding doors moment. I said yes to absolutely everything. Any job offers, any little thing I could do for somebody, any interview opportunity or scrappy advice, I'd jump on it. Even if it didn't pay in dollars, it paid in experience. Which was good, because I wasn't exactly raking in buckets of cash from podcasting.

That in itself was a blessing, because no money meant the stakes were pretty low. For me, personally, they'd never been higher, but the world's economy wasn't going to collapse if I made a podcast and nobody listened to it. Since I was doing it for free, there were no expectations on me except for what I put on myself. And I have to say, that's really valuable when you're trying to get into a new career or try something new. When there are no expectations, you can't fall short of someone else's goal for you. You can say yes without fear. I mean, if no one is paying you, it's not like they can give you the sack. And if no one can sack you, then you can follow your own path. You can do whatever the fuck you want. You can try weird things. You can fail. You can be shit. You can be brilliant.

No expectations means no limits. No limits means that once you've got an idea of what you want from life, you can go out and get it. 'It' can be whatever 'it' is, which is how you work out what it's supposed to be in the long run. That was a massive thing to me. The freedom to experiment is one of the greatest things about going through life. If you make a habit of saying yes to setting goals that might be too hard or out of your reach, you can start to get a little closer towards them. If you don't hit them dead-on, that's okay.

For Sam, the biggest takeaway from the 'yes approach' has been learning to be comfortable with fluidity – knowing that your whole life, or even just how you feel about it, might change direction at any time. And that it's not something to be worried about, but something to be excited about.

Map your mindset

There's a visualisation exercise Sam recommends trying. She suggests putting together a bit of a mind map of your experiences to help you better understand them. You can actually draw a map if it helps – I'm a visual guy, so I recommend it. But basically, think about the last 18 months of your life – what you've done, where you've been, what you've tried – then ask yourself some questions:

- What are all the different things you've said yes to?
- Out of them, which one did you really like?
- Why did you like it?

Was it because you were exposed to new people and new ideas? Or because it gave you time to yourself? Or put you in a physical domain that was new to you? Or challenged you in a way you found really rewarding?

There's no wrong answer and unlimited right ones. What this exercise gives you is a bit of a map of where your experiences have taken you and inspiration on where your path might want to go next.

'After you've said yes to so much, you get a better understanding of how you feel when you do different things,' explains Sam. 'You can kind of identify what you like and where you want to go.'

Which is exactly what happened to me. If you'd told me I'd be in this career when I was an anxious, eager kid whose one big dream was to play footy, I would have laughed. Who would have thought that with my background I'd end up having these deep and meaningful conversations with all kinds of different people? That there was an audience out there hungry for real, honest chat between a curious guy and these fascinating people who come in for a natter?

Making moves

One of my first real-life encounters with a high-achieving, growth mindset personality remains one of the best examples of the concept to this day. An absolute rare unit who has achieved extraordinary things despite a world literally built to get in his way.

Around 2016, Dylan Alcott came to the Carlton Football Club to give us a bit of the old motivational speech. I was struck by this handsome, charismatic, talented, bubbly dude with the most positive, amazing mindset. He was very inspiring – not just for his origin story, but for the fact that he was the epitome of a bloke who just had a crack. Just absolutely went hammer and tongs at life and won and continues to win. Dylan is the pinnacle of what you can achieve if you just go, 'You know what? If you want to do something, you've just got to get on and *do* it.' That's the power that you can unlock with a high-growth, positive mindset. I've found it's one of the major factors that elevates the true champions above the rest of the field. In sports, but more importantly, in regular life.

Jumping the fence/breaking the glass ceilings

Dylan is an absolute legend in sport. In media. In pretty much every arena. This book is barely long enough to list his achievements: 2022 Australian of the Year, Paralympic Gold medal winner, multiple tennis championships, TV and radio host extraordinaire, author, motivational speaker, musical festival curator, disability advocate, thought leader, charity founder – the list goes on. So, it was an absolute honour to get him on the pod.[16] Dylan's the most impressive man in pretty much any room he enters. An unstoppable force, a dude that projects the energy that there's nothing he can't do.

'Bar one activity,' he says with a laugh. 'Walking.

'I've been in a wheelchair my whole life. I was born with a tumour the size of half a watermelon wrapped around my spinal cord. And so, I was like a nine-and-a-half-pound baby. Poor Mum,' he says.

The medical team successfully cut the tumour out, but the operation left Dylan a paraplegic. He estimates that it took up to 15 operations before the age of four to save his life. He flatlined a couple of times. 'But after that,' he says, 'all good medically, to be honest. I've been pretty lucky that I've never really been back [to hospital] since.'

The way Dylan tells it, he didn't really notice his disability as a kid, was pretty happy, confident and enjoyed who he was. Using his wheelchair, he proved himself a gun athlete early on. 'I loved playing footy. I was more of a step ladder, though, than a participant. Because vertical leap – not one of my fortes.'

In his early teens, everything changed. Suddenly, the mates who had been with him all through childhood were going out and partying. It was hard for Dylan to keep up. They became less patient with him too. 'Which was fair enough, because when you're 13 you don't go, *Oh hang on, I forgot my mate in the wheelchair back there.*'

The bullying started too. 'I got called a cripple and a spastic everywhere I went. For me, those words have a real negative connotation. I fully started believing them wholeheartedly.'

That Dylan, the kid who internalised that negative self-belief, was a world away from the handsome, charismatic man he is now. He became isolated, hated himself, didn't go to school, stayed in and played PlayStation, became obese on a diet of Doritos and Red Rooster cheesy nuggets. At that point, if you'd told him that one day he would be a globally admired athlete, he says, 'I would've told you to get fucked. Because I had no desire, no passion, but most importantly, no pride in who I was.'

Dylan had friends at school, but wasn't getting invited anywhere outside of the classroom. When he found out his good mate was having a house party without inviting him, he told himself that his mates really hated him because he was different. When he asked his older brother for advice on how to deal with not being invited, he told Dylan that he and his mates usually just jumped the fence.

'Primo, primo advice for your brother in a wheelchair,' laughs Dylan. 'Anyway, I just decided to turn up. I had four UDLs and knocked on the door. My mate opened it with this shocked look on his face.'

The mate apologised for not inviting him, explaining that he didn't know if Dylan would have been able to get up the two steps up to his house. He'd been too embarrassed to talk about Dylan's disability and ask him the question directly.

'More important than that,' Dylan explains, '*I* was embarrassed to talk about my disability with him. I used to shy away from it because I wasn't proud of who I was. So, it was a sliding doors moment. From that day on I decided to never let my disability get in the way of anything I wanted to do. I needed to be proud of it. And that's when my life changed.'

Dylan realised that the more you talk about uncomfortable or sensitive things – race, religion, sexual orientation, disability, whatever it is – the more normal it becomes. While disability is one of the least normalised parts of society, he decided he wasn't going to sit around waiting for the world to change. He knew he had to meet it halfway and find a way to smash the invisible walls holding people in – what he calls 'the glass ceilings of the world'.

'You've gotta buy a ticket to win the raffle,' he says. 'If you see someone you like at a bar who you think is good looking, go ask 'em on a fucking date. If you wanna get a job, pay rise or promotion, tell someone. They're not gonna find you if you're just sitting there. Whatever you put out in the world tends to make things happen. You gotta make your own luck and put yourself in a situation where things can come to you.'

For Dylan, his meteoric rise started with sport. It brought back his fitness and with it, his drive to achieve and change the world. It also brought in the social aspect of sport which he says is one of his favourite parts of the whole experience – the way it brings people of all walks of life together, people who might otherwise have nothing in common, but find common ground. It's also a way to inspire others through your example.

He tells the story of going to a wheelchair tennis tournament in rural Australia and seeing a guy park his car, kiss his wife and kids goodbye and then leave his car using a wheelchair. It was a revelation. Until then he'd never known that wheelchair users could drive cars or start families. Watching him, Dylan had a series of important realisations. 'He drives a car. He has a missus. He has kids, does that mean he fucks?' Dylan laughs. 'I'm telling you, I didn't know we could do that shit, man.'

All these steps built the growth mindset which made Dylan the champion he is today. 'I'm so proud of being disabled. I love it. If I could do stem cell therapy and walk, you could not pay me enough. You could pay me $10 million, I wouldn't do it. Because Dylan in a wheelchair is a much better version of any other Dylan I could have been.'

After a stint playing wheelchair tennis, Dylan played his first game of wheelchair basketball in 2004. He made his World Championship debut two years later for which his team won a bronze medal. He continued to dominate the sport and won gold for Australia as part of the Australian Rollers Wheelchair Basketball team in 2008. In 2014, he returned to wheelchair tennis and the rest is history.

Dylan's excelled in multiple sports, but to watch him play tennis is a masterclass. The dude is an absolute weapon on a tennis court. He's won a truckload of grand slams and made history in 2021 when he became the first Australian to win a Golden Slam – all four Majors and Paralympic Gold in the same year. He once set the world record for the longest continuous playing of wheelchair tennis, playing non-stop for 24 hours to raise funds for charity.

I cannot imagine the sort of physical ability that requires, let alone the mental strength you'd have to have in the first place. Tennis is such an incredibly mentally taxing game. I can't think of another sport that requires more intense mental isolation over such a long period of time. There are no teammates, no caddy like in golf, no clock. I watch a match on TV and the realisation that it could theoretically go on forever makes me sweat. At the elite level, a game will continue until one player breaks and makes a mistake. The mindset you'd have to build to sustain that level of endurance must be extraordinary.

'Yeah, you become a fucking crazy person out there,' says Dylan when I ask him about it. What other sport do you compete in all by yourself, for three to four hours at a time, having a breakdown in the sun? You can see on the players' faces that they are completely sunk in their own world of focus.

'It is very much about mindset,' says Dylan. 'Do you know who wins any sporting match? It's not the person who plays the best, it's the person who thinks the most clearly.'

Clarity of thought

We can't all be Samantha Gash or Dylan Alcott, but there are ways to actively manage your mindset and help you achieve in the day to day. That's how you work out what you want out of life, and better yet, how to go get it.

At school I used to get in trouble because I could never pay attention and wouldn't stop talking to people when I was supposed to be quiet. Now, that's my job. In footy, one of my favourite parts of the whole experience was the locker-room banter. But it wasn't until I adopted a growth mindset that I realised that the banter, not the on-field action, was the real career path for me. That realisation only came after I adopted the mindset to have a go, make it part of my personality and start making moves.

Mindset Toolkit

- Mindset is fundamental. It's something you can get better at managing with practice.
- 'Just relax' is bad advice, but there are ways to manage stress and help calm down.
- Our brains are wired for stress responses. It's not because you're weak, it's not because you are struggling – your mind is wired to go there.

- Meditation is giving your attention a job. It's like taking the rubbish out for your mind.
- There are heaps of simple breath meditations, but one that works for me is the '3, 4, 5'. You breathe in for three seconds, hold for four seconds, and breathe out for five seconds. Try it. It trips that mechanism that's telling you to panic and helps calm you down.
- Our A game is when we are firing on all cylinders, feel calm and can think clearly. Our B game is when our state of mind is preventing us from bringing our best to a situation. Meditation and breathwork can help you switch from your B game to your A game and return to a more chilled state.
- Your emotions aren't who you are, just what you're feeling. If you've got a decision to make that gives you big feelings, wait 24 hours before you react to it. The situation won't change, but your feelings might.
- A growth mindset starts with being open to new things. The more new experiences you say 'yes' to, the more opportunities will open up. If you identify what you like, it's easier to work out where you want to go.
- Try making a 'mindset map' like Sam Gash. Make a list of different things you've tried in the past 18 months, work out which of them you liked and why you liked them, and use that as a starting point to look for clues about where to go next in life.
- You've got to buy a ticket to win the raffle. Whatever you put out in the world tends to make things happen. You gotta make your own luck and put yourself in a situation where things can come to you.

SUCCESS

CHAPTER 11
WHAT DO YOU EVEN WANT OUT OF LIFE?

I used to think that you measured success by the things you could count. Like my worth was counted by the more goals I kicked, or the more famous I could be. Or by having the nicest house, the coolest car. All those sorts of things. But those are just things. There's nothing wrong with them, but chasing them isn't success as I define it today. It's just a process of accumulation. Which means there's no end to it, really. Obviously you need to work and get money to put a roof over your head and feed yourself, but once you start buying these things to signal that you're 'successful', you can spend an infinite amount of money. Now, I've turned my thinking around on it a bit.

That goes for other types of success too. I love making podcasts and obviously I want the shows I make to be successful. When I first started making podcasts, the goal was to make *Dyl & Friends* the number one podcast in the charts and hearts of listeners. Which we did, by the way, and that's great, but reaching that goal has given me a more nuanced understanding of what I truly want. Deep down, I never actually wanted to create the biggest podcast in Australia. When the thing you want to become successful at gets bigger, so do the responsibilities.

As rapper Biggie Smalls says, 'Mo money, mo problems.' He wasn't lying. I've found that as your projects become bigger, so do your problems. And bigger problems need bigger solutions. Which means you have to work even harder to keep levelling up, which means less time to spend doing other things. When really, if you looked at the big picture, the things you're being taken away from might actually be your definition of success.

If you looked at the big picture, the things you're being taken away from might actually be your definition of success.

For me, I've realised that success isn't being a gun on the footy field or the podcast charts, although both those things have been important to me at different life stages. I see it like this: success can be broken down into little key factors. Money, prestige and respect are all factors, for sure. But also important, maybe more important, is the opportunity to use my time on this planet to do the things I really want to do.

What is my definition of success?

A few years back, I was all about the hustle. When I first set up my office I would get to work at eight in the morning and get home at eight at night. All day I'd sit in my office, grinding away. I was trying to get my podcast off the ground, with no time for anything else. That was probably a time when I was working too much.

While the business was doing really well and it was all really good for the bank account, I was miserable. I think of that time compared to when I was in Sydney. Back then I had the least amount of money I'd ever lived on, but was absolutely bouncing off the walls with excitement about being alive. The money had nothing to do with the happiness. Money doesn't hurt, sure, but in the end, it isn't connected to any of that stuff that is really going to make you happy.

Even the meaning of success at work is different for me. I love seeing the poddy shoot up the charts, of course, but that's not the main thing. Success to me means having an impact – being able to connect and create meaningful relationships with incredible people. The podcast is an extension of that, from the guests to the audience to the team.

My favourite thing about Producey is the people I work with. Adam, Zach, both Sams, Darcy, Stef and Scott. I spend more time with my colleagues than I do with my family. So I'm really lucky to be surrounded by such awesome motivated people. As much as I say don't care about being the best, in a way I still do, because I'm competitive. I want to keep going all the time and keep pushing myself to new levels, which is fine.

But I suppose I've changed my mindset on what it is I like about it. Is it achieving the goal? Or is it the process of achieving the goal. For me, these days, it's the latter . . . the journey is more important than the destination.

Freedom is important to me too. As in, how often can I do the things I really want? I've worked out that for me, success means I have the option to play golf midweek and spend time in my garden and with my wife, Juzz, on the weekend, instead of sacrificing that time for money. More time with friends and family like that is honestly my best measure of success. Because if I kept grinding away, earning more dough but never seeing my mates, my family, or Juzz, then would I consider that being more successful? I don't think so. Maybe I'd be richer. Maybe there'd be more money in the bank and a nicer car in the driveway, but I don't think I'd be more successful.

Zen and the art of golf

For me, one measure of success could be that I built my business up to the point where I could take a work trip to the UK and hook in some golfers to have on the pod, basically as an excuse to go watch some premium golf. Funny story about how that happened.

I was working away in 2022 when I got an email from a guy asking to have coffee and talk about creating some content together. I said yes – I get those emails all the time and try to say yes when I can – but was stressed out at the time, so put it off as long as I could. I postponed a couple of times, but eventually made good on my commitment and went to meet the guy. His name was Ali Terai, the founder and CEO of Future Golf – who I later got on the pod.[17] But at our initial meeting, what started as a work chat ended up going much deeper. Soon we were discussing life, our values, all these sorts of things. After a while, he gave me an unexpected invitation.

'Mate,' he said, 'I'm going to Scotland in a few weeks for the British Open. Do you want to come?'

'Sure,' I said. 'Okay.'

It was a busy time at work – the podcast was cooking away and I had all sorts of other side commitments with the AFL and various media companies. But something, some gut feeling I couldn't quite put my finger on, told me to do it. Juzz was flat out with work at the same time, so she was cool with it too.

And it turns out that following my gut at this moment was a good call. Ultimately, as you'll soon learn, the random sequence of events with Ali reminded me of a few important lessons:

1. Say yes to life.
2. Trust your intuition.
3. Take the uncommon action.

Over there we ran into Lucas Herbert, the all-Aussie-bloke-turned-pro golfer. As we got chatting, he turned out to be the nicest guy in the world and invited us over to his place to record a podcast.[18] This was midweek, right in the middle of the most important competition in the world. This weapon on the green is trying to do his thing, yet still makes time to have a chat. It was a 'pinch yourself' moment for me, that's for sure, to meet this guy living the dream, a country boy from Bendigo with an incredible outlook on life.

'I don't want to be Tiger Woods. I don't want to be at that level,' he says, explaining that for a player to be the peak, elite, top of their sport, there's a lot of baggage that goes with that. It takes a serious toll on your family and your social life. It requires being an extraordinary athlete who's willing to make massive sacrifices. Being the best in the world takes a certain kind of selfishness. The competition is brutal. And you've got to be a certain type of person to want that.

When I chatted to Lucas, he was ranked 40th in the world, which he was stoked with.

'Let's say from here I get to 15th in the world, or fifth, or second. Is being number one in the world that much more gratifying? Is it worth the sacrifices that asks of your family, your friends?'

Outsiders think that an elite athlete's goal is supremacy. But by definition, only one person can be the very best. Meaning, there's also room for those who just want to compete and embrace the game and lifestyle for what it is.

Take my good friend, AFL player Chris Judd. Juddy is the GOAT, inarguably a giant of the game. I love Chris Judd, but I never wanted to *be* Chris Judd. Once I understood how hard he worked, how much he sacrificed – his diet, time, body – to reach his level of performance, I began to see the appeal of being a fringe player. To try and be him, train like him, play in his shoes, it would have destroyed me.

Lucas Herbert? I get the impression he figured that out *waaay* faster than I did. Of course, he's aiming to the best he can be. But he also knows that the difference between him-being-him versus him-being-Tiger-Woods and unable to leave his house without the whole world knowing just isn't worth the sacrifice. Lucas is happy being top 50 in the world and having this incredible life where he travels with his family, friends and team, earning great money doing the things he loves.

'If I get to 40th as my best, 15th, fifth, second, first, whatever it is – I'm happy with that. Happy with the life that I've lived. I'll have no regrets.'

Obviously, when you're playing golf at an elite level there's lots of money involved, but that's not his priority. 'Money becomes a big thing. But . . . I come from Bendigo. Hypothetically, if I'm offered $200 million or $20 million, those two figures are going to change my life in the same way. On a scale, it's not like $180 million is going to make my life $180 million better . . . Bendigo boys, we sit in the pub and tell stories. We're not sitting there showing off the things we've been able to buy.'

When I ask Lucas to describe the epitome of success, he says he pictures himself at 60 in a rocking chair waiting for five o'clock to roll around so he can start smashing beers and telling stories with the other old folk. He gives his sport 100 per cent and doesn't want any regrets about not trying his guts out, but says that if he can reflect on his career, knowing he did his best while having a great time, that will be the real win. 'To look back and be able to say, "You know what, that was my golf career. It was everything I wanted it to be and I was having an absolute blast at the time." If I can say that at the end of the day, I will sit there very happily telling stories for the rest of my life.'

Gratitude as a super power

The older I become, the more I realise that's it. Being grateful for what you have, what you've been given. That epiphany I had walking from my scooter back to my house in Sydney was the real start of it for me. I realised that even though my AFL career was coming to end, everything would be okay.

There was no one big factor that led me to that point of acceptance and excitement about the future, but one of the most important things was gratitude. After that fateful chat with Bolts about my negativity, I'd begun to switch up the way I saw the world. From then on, I began actively looking for things to be grateful for – the Blues for taking a punt on me, the Giants for letting me go, all of it. Gratitude is a habit, something I've learned to practise over the years. Like any habit, it's something I picked up, then forgot about, then remembered, and so on and so on, until it finally began to stick.

There was no one big factor that led me to that point of acceptance and excitement about the future, but one of the most important things was gratitude.

It all started with a sheep's brain on a footy camp.

This one pre-season footy camp a performance psychologist was brought in by the club. He wanted to teach us how our brains work and brought in a sheep's brain for us to study. A literal, actual sheep's brain, out on the table on display. We were instructed to poke around parts of the brain with toothpicks, labelling them and explaining what they did: here's the frontal cortex, there's the pineal gland, this does that. That sort of thing.

My clearest memory from all that prodding and poking around is the part of the brain where grit comes from. I can't tell you what that actual 'bit' is, but from there comes the ability to control, endure and push yourself forward. It also happens to be the part activated by feelings of gratitude. Now, by actively practising gratitude – consciously taking time to consider the people and things in your life that make you feel grateful – you change your brain chemistry. And because the two live in the same centre, you can hack your way to increasing your grit by practising gratitude.

It's simple maths, really. More grit means more determination. More determination creates more successful people. Successful people feel more grateful. It's a self-fulfilling thing – the gratitude makes you more likely to grit your teeth and say, 'Fuck it, life's awesome, let's go for it.'

So, there I was, poking this wobbly sheep's brain with a toothpick, hearing this chat about grit and gratitude, and I had this profound realisation. If you look at your typical gun AFL rookie, they're just so grateful to be picked, to be there with the boots on, that they excel on the field. They try extra hard because they don't take it for granted. Where for me, that was the opposite of my experience. I'd taken my selection for granted and neglected to be grateful for this incredible opportunity. It was no wonder the other guys were overtaking me in terms of determination.

From that moment I started to actively practise gratitude. I'd regularly stop to think about what I was grateful for: my mum and dad, my sister, my partner Juzz, my mates, my team, my footy . . . on and on. Once I started to join the dots, I realised I had so, so much to be grateful for. I was just super grateful for it all.

Number 43

A specific example of this is my guernsey number. In footy, when a player is recruited, they get assigned a number. Generally, the numbers are assigned as a player is drafted – so the low numbers go to the high-draft picks. If you are number one on the draft, that means the recruiters wanted you more than any other player. Numbers two, three, four, up to 10, are the most highly sought-after draft picks.

Naturally, the higher numbers are less desirable. If your number is up near 50, that means you've been rookied in after the really hot players have already been assigned their numbers. No kid is going into the game with the desire to have a guernsey number in the 40s.

When I was brought into Carlton, I was assigned number 7. That was a big honour, a huge show of respect for me from the club – they didn't have to do that and it meant they really believed in me. There have been many legendary number 7s in AFL, so that number never really sat right with me. Seven is a number for the best of the best, and with my footy going downhill as the years passed, I never felt I could own it. I'd hoped early on that I'd grow into it, but no matter how hard I tried, I just never felt like I really deserved it.

When I got to the Giants, I was given the number 43, the second highest (therefore second worst) number at the club, way down the end of the locker room, where the rookies who only just squeaked onto the list reside.

I fucking loved it.

By then, I'd had my sheep's brain epiphany and gratitude had become something I practised regularly. I was so grateful to have that 43 on my back. I loved that it was a high number, I loved that it wasn't the number a young player would want. It was mine. It came with knowing I hadn't taken an easy ride to get there and was lucky to be in the AFL at all.

Dylan Buckley, number 43. I embraced it 100 per cent. My footy didn't necessarily improve in that guernsey, but the quality of everything else in my life did. I embraced the mentality of guernsey 43 and all that meant and I went for it. I loved it because it was mine, because it was my story still being written. Number 43 – bit of a list clogger, but so fucking grateful for the opportunity.

Now, every day, I practise gratitude. For me gratitude is about being fully present, not so much going home each night and writing down the things I'm grateful for that day or in my life, but more about appreciating the moment I'm in, in the actual moment. When I'm at work, the amazing team I get to work with: fucking amazing. On the weekend, when I'm just chilling out with Juzz: unbelievable. I tell myself, *Yeah, this is it, I'm grateful for this.* In real time, it's sometimes hard to believe that this is my life, that everything has brought me to this situation, to this moment.

I've found for myself that being grateful is like any good habit. It comes and goes, ebbs and flows. Sometimes you lose it – it's there one minute and then it's not – but the more you can remember to pull that trigger in your brain when something good happens, and actively identify the feeling as gratitude, the easier it gets. The more it comes up, the easier it becomes to trigger that feeling.

The crazy thing is, it has a tangible, real-life effect. The day I started to concentrate on being more grateful for my good luck, my luck got better. Practising gratitude had the knock-on effect of making more good things happen in my life. Or it seemed that way. It's possible that I was just realising how many good things actually happened to me and then was receptive to more good things happening. Which is really cool.

I guess it comes down to this question. Is gratitude really working? Or am I just becoming more present to all the cool things in my life? The best part is, there's no wrong answer, because you're getting the same outcome anyway.

So that's how I practise gratitude on a daily basis. It's about being present and at the end of the day, looking at and appreciating all the things I'm grateful for. Every night I lie in bed and think about the best things that happened in the day. If there are things that didn't happen the way I wanted them to, I take some time to think about the better things that could happen tomorrow. Either way, it's been a success. That's what gratitude does for you.

The four-burner theory

American writer David Sedaris uses this 'Four Burner' analogy for work–life balance.[19] It's something he got from a friend, who got it from a business seminar. So, useful in all situations, and now I'll pass it on to you. He imagines life as a gas stove with four burners, each representing a major area in our life – family, friends, work, health. In his theory, we only have enough gas to run three of the four burners at one time.

So right out of the gate, I guess he's saying it's impossible to keep everything in balance. But still, we try. So, we keep three burners running at an even heat. But then you injure yourself, or your wife gets pregnant, or your mate's getting married, so you power up that burner, sacrificing heat to the others. Want to hit big career goals? Turn up the heat on work, knowing it will take gas from another burner – your family, friends, or health. If you really want to crank something you have the option of turning one cooker on full gas and leaving the others dead cold.

It's a visual way to imagine the trade-offs we make in life. Do you want to work so hard that your health suffers? Or are you willing to lose contact with your mates in order to put in late nights at the office? Or do you want to have a full life with family and friends, but put work on the back burner, which means you can't be as ambitious with your career? From my own experience, and as I've learned from speaking to others . . . you can't *always* be comfortable trying to keep the four burners in balance. Sometimes, you have to fire one full out, burn it as hard as you can. Sometimes, that's the only way to get things done. And when you do, you know eventually it will burn out. It's inevitable. So then, you're forced to come back and reassess. No one can tell when is or isn't the right time to invest all your energy in one burner, or when you should pull back. You only learn this by doing. It's a tough choice at times, but success is all about making those choices.

Goalposts shift and that's a good thing

Not every combination of burners is going to work for everyone and your priorities will change through life. I've definitely gone through periods where I've had the work burner turned up way too high and other areas of my life have suffered. At a certain point, I realised that I was sitting all day staring at screens and started to wonder what I was doing. I found myself looking back on my time in Sydney, where I had literally four friends, played footy in the fringes and didn't do anything on the weekend besides what I wanted. Life had been so simple. Now, in business for myself, it was exhausting.

Was spending all those hours killing myself making my business better? Was working 10 hours a day really making me more productive than working eight? Or could I possibly come in and work for four hours and still get the same amount done? Whose rules was I following that said my arse had to be on a seat all day instead of working the hours that made me an efficient unit? I was chasing my goal, but was I doing it in a way that would result in my dream coming true? If not, then whose dream was I actually chasing?

When I went all-in on podcasting, I had no idea what I was doing. For a while there I was faking it while I was making it – inventing the rules as I went and chasing success. I was very lucky, and worked with some absolute heroes, and together we built something even better than I'd imagined. My absolute dream job.

But it took me ages to realise that even a dream job is only part of life. Other things are just as important. More important. And most important of all – those things will change through life. What you want out of life at 30 is different to 20, just like what you want at 20 is different to what you wanted at 10. Otherwise you'd end up with a bunch of old guys sitting around drinking Vodka Cruisers and playing Fortnite.

The goalposts will shift, and that's part of the caper. I think it pays to regularly check in with yourself and work out if you're investing your time in the things that will really make you happy. Family, friends, work, golf – it's all good, but make sure you know what your goals are, and that you're getting the ball up the right end of the field.

CHAPTER 12

GETTING GOOD AT GOALS

Nick Riewoldt is good at goals. He hits his mark. Literally. Rooey holds the record for most marks in VFL/AFL history. He was the much-loved skipper of St Kilda Football Club for close to a decade, played a few premierships and was awarded St Kilda's Best and Fairest, the Trevor Barker Award *six* times. Since retiring from footy, he's become a multi-hat media personality, appearing on several shows including a champion run on *Celebrity MasterChef,* which is where my mum thinks he did his best work. Personally, I reckon his visit to the pod beat that, but hey, I might be biased.[20]

I don't know if anyone else's mum is like this, but I spend a fair bit of our time together helping her with her devices. She'll come to me saying, 'Oh, Instagram's not working,' so, while

I'm updating it for her, I'll look through who she's following and it's all these people from reality shows that aired seven years ago. Which is how one day I noticed that there on my mum's feed was the man, the legend, Nick 'Rooey' Riewoldt, in his MasterChef gear.

The man embodies high achievement and getting the most out of life. So when I got the chance to ask him about his own approach to setting goals, I jumped at it.

'There's no secret, no magic formula,' he said. 'You either do the work or you don't. All the great players, they do the work. Some guys can bob up for a season, a really good season, and then you wonder why they're never able to recreate it . . . because you've just got to continue to do the work.'

But what does that actually mean?

'Once you've set them, how you get about hitting your goals is more complicated. But it starts with the goal you set. It has to be something that, in your mind, is achievable in the first place. Otherwise, you bang your head up against a brick wall. You do the work and get disappointed, and disappointment is a hard thing to overcome continually.'

I know it well. I spent eight years banging my head against the wall – first the bricks at Princes Park, then in Western Sydney. As one footy goal after another (literally and then metaphorically) slipped through my fingers, it got harder and harder for me to get sight of the champion vision that had brought me to footy in the first place. It's hard to maintain the sort of work ethic that elite footy requires if you're continually missing your goals.

According to Rooey, it's a matter of setting your sights on the ultimate goal, then breaking it down into smaller, achievable wins. The smaller wins fuel you on to the bigger ones and pump your tyres on your way to greater things. A team wins a premiership one kick at a time. Conversely, the little misses and times you lose become easier to recover from. Losing a grand final is gutting for any footballer. It's easier to mentally recover from an early season loss and rally your strength from there.

Rooey says that identifying who you want to be, what you want to achieve and where you want to get to, are the keys to defining your goals. 'And then, what are the specific actions that are going to give you the *best chance* of succeeding, even while there's *no guarantee* of success?'

Then, it's a matter of taking those actions and working out how to make them a reality. 'I did a lot of work early in my career just on positive affirmations,' says Rooey, who was injured eight weeks into his first proper season and came into his second year champing at the bit. 'I just wanted to be really good.'

He had conversations with a couple mentors at the club who helped him clarify what he wanted to be as a player. A big man, an absolutely towering figure, he knew he was built different to a lot of the key forwards that were coming through at the time. So he needed to develop a playing style that would dominate the field.

'The underpinning line that I came back to is, *Well, I wanna be the hardest-working forward in the game.*'

So, that was his affirmation. Rooey got a notebook and wrote it out hundreds of times a day. He still has notebooks from his second year on the team, full of that one thing written thousands of times, page after page. *Nick Riewoldt is the hardest-working forward in the game.*

'I would talk about myself in the third person, which is a bit cringe, but that's what affirmations are,' he says.

Beneath the affirmation he would write down two or three actions that would underpin that, really specific actions that would tie into being the hardest-working forward in the game. *Burn my opponent with explosive leads. Get up and beat them back.*

Young Nick Riewoldt would write an affirmation down and repeat it and repeat it and repeat it and repeat it until, after a year or two, people started saying, 'Nick Riewoldt is the hardest-working forward in the game.'

These weren't skills he walked through the door with, but he worked at it until they were, and the work itself became 'a bit of a badge of honour. Once people started reaffirming what I'd been telling myself, it just fuelled that desire to keep doing it and get better at it and refine it. In the end, that became my identity. And that came from identifying my own strengths, drilling down on them, reaffirming them, and then acting them out.'

Setting good goals

In my last year at GWS, when I understood that I would be leaving footy and was working out what the fuck I was going to do next, I wrote my thoughts down. Literally, in a notebook I still have, I wrote down a list of what I wanted and where I wanted to be. These included a list of things that I could see as potential futures:

- A job in radio.
- An opportunity in television.
- Podcasting to be my full-time job.

To those career three, I added around six life goals. Then, at the end of the next year, I went back to the list and . . . they had all come true. Every single one of them! (Well, except for the most important one, which I'll get into more a bit later in this book.) Every one of the possible futures I'd visualised had actually happened. I got a job in radio – a bit of a fucking disaster, but it happened. I got an opportunity in TV, doing some interviews and a bit of content for the AFL and Fox Footy. Just a bit of light banter sort of thing, and I'm so grateful for the opportunity, but I had to turn the burner down on that a bit as the podcasting really started to pick up speed. Next minute, I was working fulltime in podcasting.

At the end of that year, I couldn't believe how well everything was going. Except for that one thing. The one thing that didn't come true in that year and which was so important to me that it was really getting me down. I became so obsessed with it, but looking back now, I understand that if I had gotten it right away then it would have become the centre of my whole life and everything else might not have happened: I wouldn't have done the radio job, or had the appetite for risk that I needed to start the podcast, or to grab all the weird opportunities that came my way.

All up, the exercise was a good lesson. I learned that ultimately, while it's important to have goals and places you want to go, it pays to not be too specific on how you get there. If you've got a fair idea of where you want to be, but are flexible enough to take detours along the way, you might be pleasantly surprised at what shows up around the corner.

Which makes me think it's time for another beautifully crafted Dylan Buckley original driving analogy. Take the drive from Sydney to Melbourne. There's an inland highway that goes straight there. You can get your car up to the speed limit and fang it all the way there in eight hours, if you really want. But it's a fucking boring drive. Truly, one of the dullest in the world. But if you take the time to pull over once in a while and go visit some weird little town, it's going to be a much better trip. Even if all you get is gastro from a pie from a small-town servo, at the end of the day, at least you got a pie.

The same goes for life. I haven't loved the outcome of every little side road I've taken in life, but I'm grateful for the experience. That thing that I wrote down, and wanted more than anything, happened two years after the rest, and by then I was actually ready for it. I looked back at that notebook then and thought, *Wow, look at all the incredible stuff that happened on the way to the final goal.* It's pretty cool.

Take the long road

I think of Ryan Shelton as an example. By any conventional marker of success, he was one. Ryan made his name as a writer and comedian in the Australian entertainment industry, which isn't exactly a cakewalk. I grew up on a steady diet of the shows he worked on, including *Hamish & Andy* and *Real Stories* and Chris Lilley's *We Can Be Heroes*. He's worked as a comedian all over the shop, been on *Rove* and hosted radio shows on the big commercial networks.

But despite all that, he wasn't stoked about his success. He struggled with insecurity and the feeling that he hadn't reached his own expectations. Those feelings whacked him in the head one day, while reading *The Courage to Be Disliked* by Fumitake Koga and Ichiro Kishimi – a Japanese philosophy book that explores how to brush off social pressures and trust in your own self-worth.[21] When Ryan came on *Dyl & Friends* as a guest, we discussed how that book changed his life.[22] For the first time, he really thought about what happiness would mean to him and how he was setting the goals he had in life.

'Not that I was necessarily unhappy or anything, but what this book had to say just ticked all these boxes for me. I started thinking about my own life and I started wondering what I was really doing here.'

Ryan began to think more deeply about his career, what he'd done so far and what he really wanted in the future. He'd had success, but not enough of it. The thing he'd always really wanted more than anything, was to have his own TV show that he would write and be the star of. It had been his lifelong goal. To have his own Seinfeld-style show that everybody loved. He thought that once he had that then he would have achieved his goal and would be happy.

'Actually, I hadn't really thought about the happiness part of it,' he says. 'I just thought, well, that's what I want. I guess that's what anyone like me wants.'

Until that moment, he'd put a lot of time and mental energy into getting a TV show, but this was the first time he'd thought about how he would feel if he got everything he supposedly wanted.

'So, I really visualised myself on stage at the Emmys,' he said, with a bit of an embarrassed laugh. 'I'm on stage at the Emmys accepting the award from Will Ferrell, because in this scenario he's a huge fan and obviously wants to present it himself. And there's Jerry Seinfeld in the front row, giving me a standing ovation, going, "You've done it! Well done. Brilliant! I love you! I'm Jerry Seinfeld!"'

And while picturing himself in the moment, Ryan had an epiphany. He realised that he didn't feel anything. The scene didn't make his heart race, or make him nervous, or excited, or any of it. At the end of the day, he realised, he didn't actually care. Which was a bit of a problem, he thought, because if he wasn't stoked at the prospect of success, if he wasn't actually going to care about it when he got it, then why was he even chasing it?

I'm going for the wrong thing here, Ryan remembers thinking. It was a moment of self-realisation, followed by another realisation that he didn't quite know what to do with it. He ended up reaching out to Hugh van Cuylenburg, founder of The Resilience Project, whom he'd befriended a few years earlier.[23] *Hi mate, hope you're well*, he messaged. *I was wondering if we could catch up? Cheers, Ryan.*

They met up, and after a couple of minutes of pleasantries, Ryan came to the point. 'I feel really lost at the moment,' he said.

The way Hugh tells it, Ryan had turned up a little shell-shocked by his epiphany. He shared everything he was feeling about the future he'd realised he didn't want. Hugh was a little shocked by his rawness, describing it as one of the most vulnerable conversations he'd ever had from a standing start. It bonded the two almost immediately.

Soon the men were meeting for coffee once a week to talk about whatever issues they had going on in their lives. The more Hugh got to know Ryan, the more he understood that no matter how great someone's life appears from afar, no one is living the perfect existence. Here was a guy who was, without doubt, a success, the sort of guy Hugh had always looked up to and imagined was leading a creatively fulfilled, financially minted life. The truth was a lot more complicated, humbling and reassuring. Ryan struggled with shame, high expectations and the fear of failure, just like everybody else.

As they kept talking, the two new mates confirmed their suspicions that the relationship between success, failure, ambition and happiness was much more messy and complicated than guys in our culture are generally brought up to believe. For Ryan, that hunch was underscored when he read Andre Agassi's autobiography, where upon reaching the pinnacle of competitive tennis, winning Wimbledon, the tennis legend found that it didn't automatically make him happy. Agassi's was essentially the bigger, higher-stakes version of what Ryan had realised about himself.

'Long story short, he gets everything that he supposedly ever wanted and doesn't give a shit. So, I read that book and was like, okay, this is clearly a common thing for people.'

Hugh and Ryan's friendship eventually grew into *The Imperfects* podcast, a place where outwardly successful people share that they are, in fact, imperfect. That success doesn't magically turn into happiness and the way you define success over your lifetime is going to change. To use a bit of a footy metaphor: Just because the goal is a long way away, doesn't mean you should stand still. Keep moving, keep the ball in play, and above all, enjoy your time on the field. Because if you're not enjoying yourself, despite it being hard sometimes, then why is this the game you've chosen?

Success is personal. It's individual. Unique. Like you. Nobody can tell you what success looks like to you except you. Although, a lot of people you talk to aren't going to believe me on that and they'll argue it with the best of intentions. Which is fair. As we've covered earlier in this book, you should be open to advice from everywhere. Everyone has something to teach you. In the end though, only you can know what success looks like to you. And it just might take some time to figure it out.

Success Toolkit

- What does 'success' mean to you? Money? Fame? Followers? My definition of success has changed over time. For me, freedom is the most important thing now.
- Success is all about finding balance. Work out what your priorities are and make sure you're not sacrificing the things that really matter to find your goals.
- Try visualising what it would feel like to reach your goal. Does the idea excite you? If not, why not? Make sure you're setting your own goals and not living out someone else's dream.
- Only you can truly work out what success means to you.
- Affirmations are a bit cringe, but they work. Once you've worked out what your goals are, write them down. It's the first step to making them real in the world. Once you've written them down, start moving.
- Don't stress if you fail at first. Everyone does, that's part of it. Fail hard, fail early, fail often, and by the time you reach your goal, the experiences will have made you ready for success.

COMMUNICATION

CHAPTER 13

HONEST CHAT

Dropping everything to have a chat has always been my default mode, ever since primary school. I used to get into trouble for it then, and later told off at footy for bantering instead of hitting the gym. Now it's literally my job, and I love it, but I wasn't always very good at communication.

So, let's go back in time a little bit, to the story I told at the very start of this book. When I was watching TV and saw a bloke talking about breaking down the old-fashioned models of masculinity that weren't working anymore. Remember him? I sure do. His name is Tom Harkin. He's a thought leader who's spent a long time figuring out how human beings work and how individuals and groups can transform themselves. One of his passion projects was founding Tomorrow Man, to start the conversation about masculinity, challenging the traditional stereotypes of what 'being a man' means.

Being a hard nut and emotionally shut down are typical examples; images of manhood that I inherited, to some extent. Things are changing faster every day, but back when I was a teenager and promising footy player, my identity was all set out for me. Without ever stopping to ask myself, *Is this actually me?* I fell into the stereotypical alpha-male set of behaviours. Such as the idea of 'strength' being something you were good at, a physical skill. *I'm a strong rover. I have strong ball skills,* etc. Later on I learned that 'strength' can be anything that makes you feel powerful. For me, that means being open and vulnerable with my emotions, the exact opposite of what I'd been trained to do as a young man.

Strength can be anything that makes you feel powerful. For me, that means being open and vulnerable with my emotions.

So, pretending to be a tough nut was really detrimental to my sense of identity. Because to be honest, I'm a really emotional person. Always have been. As a kid, I'd be watching movies with my family, sitting down on the couch next to my sister and realise I was about to start crying. I could be watching *Good Will Hunting* or fucking *Shrek,* but something would happen on screen that would make me well up. *Oh fuck,* I'd realise, *I don't know what to do here.* So I'd stand up and tell my family, 'I've gotta go to the bathroom for a second.' Then I'd go stand in the bathroom blinking back the tears and wait for the emotion to go away.

As I've gotten older, I've come to realise that my intense emotions are a strength. For me, probably the biggest. I'm in touch with my feelings and I'm moved to tears pretty much all the time. I cry when I'm sad. When good things happen. I cry when I think about Juzz and the road we're on together. One day I'm gonna nail a clutch putt on a difficult green and you can put money on me having a bit of the old celebratory waterworks.

I'm cool with that now. It doesn't make me less of a man. Actually, it makes me feel tougher. When I need a bit of grit and determination I know I can turn to my emotions because the sheer strength of them revs me up. From a certain point of view, crying is my superpower. But I didn't embrace that side of myself for so long because of this dumb-shit idea of masculinity. I had it all backwards and thought of my strength as a weakness. It took a lot of work to undo that and realise where my true power lay.

But at age 25, that realisation was a long way off. There I was watching Tom Harkin talking about blokes needing to talk about their feelings on this show and I found myself sitting on the couch crying. One minute I was happily eating corn chips and the next I was having a full existential crisis. *What the fuck is going on right now? Who the fuck am I?*

I ended up sending Tom an email. The grammar was so garbled it was barely English, so I don't know how he understood it, but he wrote back, which was good of him. Later on, when I started working in media, he was one of the first guys I asked onto the pod. A crucial figure in my life, he inspired me to start a lot of the inner work I've done on myself. So, when I got the opportunity to talk to him about the work he does with men, young and old, it was a brilliant chat. He speaks with authority and from experience, his thick Aussie accent forged growing up in the blokey stronghold of Frankston, Victoria.

'What's the definition of a bloke?' Tom asks us to consider. 'And who decided what is and isn't acceptable behaviour for men, anyway? The ideals that our culture told me to aspire to – unrelenting toughness, stoicism, bottling up emotions – were decided on centuries ago. They didn't work then, and they don't work now, but we're discouraged from breaking them. It scares some guys. It even makes them aggro.

'Now's the time to ask who wrote the rules,' Tom says. 'And to go and break 'em.'

Develop your range

The way to do that is to embrace what Tom calls range. 'Range is about feeling empowered, feeling equipped and not missing out on life,' he says. 'If you only give me one [identity] choice, that's not power, that's just a straightjacket.'

Range is about having more choices on how to be a person, more tools to help you take on life. Do you have the range of tools or attributes required to live a full life? Or have you only been given half the toolkit, so you only get half a life?

Tom invites us to look at the supposed 'alpha male' in our society and what his toolkit looks like. 'You've got strength, because you need to be strong at all times. Invulnerable. You need to be the guy that provides and gets it done and never fails . . . If you take that toolkit as a given and you never move out of those bounds, you're probably gonna struggle in life. Because you're like a stick with no flex. Put enough pressure on and it snaps eventually. And once it's snapped, how do you get it back together?'

The solution to inflexibility is range, which is all about looking at your life, and the tools – the skills, talents, attribute, interests – you have and calling on them when you need them. You can be a gun athlete, but that doesn't have to be your whole personality. You can like art, dirt bikes, kittens, boxing, painting your nails, emo music, trap, disco, all at the same time. You can be all or none of those things and still be considered masculine.

You can still go out there and do everything you want to do. Be the tough guy, support your family and all the rest. You can be the hardest dude around, an absolute staunch unit, and still cry during a sad movie. What are they going to do, pick a fight with you? You're the hardest dude around, remember? The trick is to be yourself, knowing that you can have stoic strength when you do need it – because there will be times when you do need it – but that it doesn't have to be your entire personality. Because that's not much of a life.

'Personally, I believe I have one life. I've got one crack and I don't wanna miss out on it,' says Tom. 'So, I wanna have it all. I want to kiss the girl, I want to have my heart broken, I want to cry on my wedding day.'

Tom says arguing about what constitutes a 'real man' isn't asking the right question. 'You gotta ask, are we getting the tools to live a full life? Do we have enough range? Don't be stuck in a claustrophobic life with one or two tools in your toolkit. Have the range, the tool that matches up with the life experience.'

One of the most important for me – I think for everyone – is communication. Learning good communication is like owning a Leatherman Multi-Tool. Once you've got one, you'll never understand how you lived without it.

'If you come at life with the ability to have those tough conversations, everything gets better. Everything,' says Tom. 'All your relationships, how you deal with problems, conflicts, sex, the ability to say what you need, to realise when you've crossed a line, to have intimate conversations, all that stuff. But most of us have never been given the training to have those chats.'

Training for the big day

Communication is one of the most important things in my life; connecting with other human beings, getting to know them, learning new facts and ways of looking at the world.

But it's not something I was born good at. It's something I had to work on and something I still work on all the time. No one is perfect at this shit. No one is the best at being vulnerable. No one is totally amazing at expressing their emotions. But the more we do it, the more comfortable we become, the better we get. It's not like the first time you open up you have to be totally vulnerable. You don't have to go and tell your deepest, darkest secrets to all your mates. You start off by just asking people how they're going and really listening to their answer. It's something you get better at with practice.

And it's important to practise with 'live ammo' says Tom. You start small and learn to communicate even when you're feeling emotional. Your heart rate is spiking, your throat is closing and you're choking up. Are you just gonna stop talking, or are you gonna learn how to talk through tears? Learning how to talk through tears is right up there in terms of life skills.

Tom compares practising better communication with training for a grand final. A footballer spends the bulk of his time training for a chance at the cup. That means working hard every day, pushing himself, testing his limits, working out what his edge is and what he's capable of. 'Then, one day there's gonna be a grand final of emotion,' says Tom. 'You've probably already had a couple of emotional grand final moments in your life where you've needed to have a strong emotional muscle to handle the intensity of that moment.'

As I write this, I've just turned 30. Half a lifetime ago, 15-year-old Dyl thought that being a gun footballer and decent guy were the only tools he needed. Those tools worked okay for a few years, but then he found himself lacking the ones he really needed to be able to cope with his anxiety. The shit that boy would go through from there, the experiences he didn't anticipate – the loss of people, arguments, broken relationships – he couldn't have had any way of knowing how to prepare for them. Those things are unfortunately inevitable. They're gonna happen throughout your life. The more we can get ready for 'em, the better.

There's been so many times where I look back and go, *Fuck, I wish I held myself a little bit different in that situation. I wish I did that differently.* But in saying that, every time a situation or conflict doesn't go well, it's an opportunity to ask how could I have dealt with it better. Yeah, sometimes we don't get the time to train for these things, but it's a skill that you just have to keep putting the work into.

When you start practising communication, it's not always going to go your way. Look at it as a growing experience and think about how much you can get out of it. Because inevitably not everything that we go through is gonna be positive. But when you take the time to communicate better, if you learn how to speak up when you need help, it's all going to be so much easier. Speaking up is one of life's great skills. The other very important one, something I've really only learned lately, is knowing when to listen.

When you take the time to communicate better, if you learn how to speak up when you need help, it's all going to be so much easier.

Male-to-female communication

I'm going to generalise a bit here, but I reckon it's safe to say that females tend to be better than males at deeper emotional communication. Our society has very patriarchal roots which carry through to today. Compared to boys, girls are taught to communicate more effectively as part of the extra work they have to do to hold the world together. So, the burden of communication tends to fall on girls from a super young age. They tend to be better at it and have to find a way to explain it to us male knuckleheads.

That's something that's really important that I don't reckon us guys think about enough. Basically, I don't think we give girls and women credit for how much work they have to do in terms of relationships and making people happy. Because it's a hell of a lot of work, and we guys don't tend to notice it because it goes on without us knowing it, and that ignorance lets us take it for granted.

I think of my mum who is just the most incredible person I've ever met in my life. It's not exactly headline news that I love my mum, I've always thought she's amazing, but the older I get the more I realise exactly how much of my world she holds up. If, at the end of the day, I could be half of the person she is in terms of kindness, empathy, grit, strength – I'd be a superhero. She's worked her whole life to give me and my sister the opportunities that have made us so happy. In everything Mum's ever done, she's put our dreams ahead of her own. When I played footy, she never missed a game. To this day, she's the number one fan and booster for my podcast. I reckon half the ratings we enjoy are thanks to her getting the good word out.

Not that I ever took her for granted, but more and more I appreciate the incredible hard work and emotional intelligence it takes to do all she does for us. Through the years, that's included some pretty challenging circumstances. Mum and Dad had their differences over the years but she's never, not once, said a bad word about him, or done anything but encourage us all to work it out as a family.

My mum and dad are both great communicators in their own separate ways. I'd always thought that I took after my dad in terms of my love of banter. He loves a convo, that's for sure. I've known him to chat happily to anyone about anything, from a homeless guy on the street to, literally, the prime minister. I love a chat too, so at first thought, you might assume that the chats I have on the poddy are a skill I've inherited from Dad. But half, probably more than half of it, actually, comes from Mum. Her approach taught me that the most important thing in all communication is listening – and that you can't listen and talk at the same time. Two ears, one mouth. It's just maths. Being *interested* in people is way cooler than trying to be *interesting*.

So, I'm very grateful to Mum for giving me that gift, the ability to turn my ears on and connect with another human being. I'm always looking for ways to communicate better. One thing I've found that really works for me is this thing Juzz introduced me to, 'love languages'.

The five love languages

The Five Love Languages is a framework for understanding the way that people give and receive love. Psychologist Gary Chapman literally wrote the book (back in 1992) as a way of classifying people's preferred modes of showing affection, being: physical touch, words of affirmation, acts of service, quality time and gift giving. They're something that Juzz talks about a lot and understanding how these different modes work has no doubt helped our relationship.

Juzz is the love of my life, the most beautiful woman in the world and we're so happy – but sometimes I annoy the fuck out of her. I am the most over-affectionate person in the world around her. Every time I see her, I just want to hug her and tell her how much I love her. If she comes home at the end of the day, our dog is much more chilled out about it than I am. Where Juzz is a much more reserved person. She's very private and is probably going to hate it when she reads this. But Juzz is incredibly cool-headed, while I'm like this golden retriever that's been in the bickies. And it's not that she loves me less, she just expresses her love differently.

The way Juzz shows love is she *does* things. She's just a real doer. Juzz will plan for us to go out for nice lunches and buy beautiful things for the house and that's how she expresses her love. When she makes us a meal, she always makes sure it's the best. If she were to cook a lasagne, she'd make sure I had the best slice, the crispy bit from the edge of the pan. Whereas if I'm cooking, I'm probably going to eat the best bit, because I wouldn't think of the meal as an expression of affection and I'd get hungry on the way to the table. I'm more like, 'Here's your dinner, a pretty ordinary pasta. Also, twenty hugs.'

So, we're always in this battle of being two people in a relationship that have very different ways of showing their love and wanting to be shown it in return. The solution is communication. Juzz had to explain love languages to me because she's had to put in boundaries. We've got rules now, like I'm only allowed to hug her three times a day. Otherwise, it just gets too much for her. I know that I just wanna hug her and just be with her because I'm an affectionate person. But the more I do that, it becomes overwhelming for her and pushes her away; Juzz needs her physical space. Do I respect these boundaries? Well, let's just say, it's a work in progress.

It was so important for me to understand that we have very different needs in the relationship and to find a way to communicate them. So, when I got a chance to ask relationship expert and sexologist Chantelle Otten about better ways to communicate with my partner, it's no surprise that love languages came up.[24]

'It's really spot on. I'm a big believer in doing love languages because I think that it actually sorts out a lot of relationship problems as well.'

Chantelle says that as a communication tool, it's a framework that lets both sides come to understand each other and to reach an agreement. So, in our case, my love language is physical touch, while Juzz's is acts of service. So, for us, good boundaries and meeting each other's needs means agreeing that I get three hugs a day, because that's what I need to feel secure, and in return, understanding that Juzz needs her space and for me to do other things that make her feel loved – acts of service. For instance, if I know she's had a bad day or been upset, straight away I'll go home, clean the house, make the bed, cook dinner. That's the biggest way that I can show love to her.

Chantelle believes in incorporating all the love languages into a relationship, but putting a preference on the one that is most important to your partner. That's how you find common ground and create quality time together. Every morning Juzz and I go for a walk with the dog, get coffee and chat, because for us both, they're activities we can't get enough of. But we only figured that out through communication.

Communication takes all sorts of forms. Love languages is just one way of looking at it and for sure, it won't be for everyone. I think there's almost a sixth love language that's typical for male–male communication, which involves giving each other shit.

Male-to-male communication

For most of my footy career, my favourite part of the whole experience was the team. At Carlton, then again at the Giants, I loved the training, the locker room and the team trips to train in random, gruelling places, because the chat was so good. Just extraordinary banter from the boys.

Footy coaches are trained to break you down and build you up again as a staunch unit, but they can take a whole season to do that, whereas I've known footballers who can do it with one line of locker room banter. Honestly, I think it's an under-appreciated art within the glorious sport of AFL. There's a lot of physical suffering that goes into making a good footy player, so banter and joking become a kind of coping mechanism. We were very good at joking around and dunking on each other, because it's a kind of love language. In the absence of those real deep conversations, banter was how we worked through the incredible emotional highs and lows of elite sport.

Let's bring in my good mate Hunter Johnson again, whose explanation of banter is spot on. He says that most of our social interactions are ways of testing our boundaries for safety. We're socialised to understand that only a certain level of sharing and vulnerability is acceptable. For young males, especially, we're trained to dance around our emotions, rather than tackling them head-on.

I think of my dog – a French bulldog and an actual living angel on earth – as a good analogy. She's not the biggest unit, but she has a lot of heart. If you've ever watched dogs playing in a park, that's a good picture of what it's like to be a young man working out your emotions through banter. You'll see two dogs meet for the first time and then sort of sniff each other out, run around, roll around and play fight. They are working out if they are safe with each other by having a sort of sparring match that's just for fun.

'That's what banter is,' Hunter explains. 'It's like, "Are we cool? Are you okay with what I've put out there? Yeah? Okay, we're good." The vulnerability gives us permission to connect and that gives that social proof that everything's okay. *I can trust you.*'

That brings us to one of the most important things I've ever learned, which is how to embrace vulnerability. When you get past the banter and into talking about something real, something that puts you in an emotionally vulnerable spot, you have no evidence that you're gonna be okay. If we push past the superficial into authentic expression, into honesty? There's a possibility that the other person might react badly, or change their mind about us. That's a real fear and it's fucking frightening. 'When you're in uncharted territory and feel there is no way that it's worth it, that's when you know you've hit your edge,' Hunter says.

Living on the edge

I was sweating bullets the first time I was ever called upon to talk about vulnerability and mental health. I couldn't even get the words 'mental illness' out of my mouth. Fast forward a couple of years and now I can't say a complete sentence without talking about vulnerability and mindset. The boys bag me out about it a lot. They make videos all the time pretending to be me. Doesn't faze me, I've got range. Bet I could demolish any of them in a crying competition from a standing start. I've gotten pretty good at being vulnerable too. I've learned that males are capable of so much more when it comes to communication with other guys, and it's so important. It's absolutely worth working on. But it's not always comfortable. In the beginning, it's actually pretty tough.

Learning to hit the edge of your comfort zone, and go beyond it, is what vulnerability is all about. It's how we grow and become better men. For me, it's one of the most important life skills you can ever learn.

The problem with traditional Aussie masculinity is that if we aren't encouraged to embrace that stuff, then we start the race of life from way back in the field. I know from my experience that the day I started actively opening myself up and being vulnerable – with girls, with other guys, with family – everything started falling into place. Things I thought were impossible challenges weren't actually that daunting when I shared them. That said, sharing is only half of being vulnerable. The other half is listening.

CHAPTER 14

VULNERABILITY AND THE LIFE-CHANGING MAGIC OF SHUTTING UP

I'm a pretty typical guy in that if you bring me a problem, I'll try and fix it. If I'm with my mates and one of us has a problem, I'll try and fix it. Say I'm out playing golf with a mate and he confides in me that he's having trouble at work, or with his partner. Whatever it is, you know that by the end of the course I've workshopped that problem from every angle. *Try this, do that, think about it this way, look at the sunny side*. It's not like I don't have problems of my own that need fixing – I've got truckloads of them – but for some reason I'm always first in line to try and fix other people's problems.

I was sitting down with my wife Juzz once and we were talking about something that was troubling her. Just everyday life problems, normal stuff, a regular night in every way.

Every time she gave me a new detail on her problem, I was on it like a contested mark, 'You should do this, I can do this other thing for you, we can fix it in this way.'

'Can you just listen to me?' Juzz said to me after a lot of unsolicited advice had been sent her way. 'Just listen. I don't need you to tell me what to do. I don't want you to give me wisdom, I don't want you to give me a plan, I just want you to *listen* to me.'

It was a Eureka moment for me. *Fuck, I don't always have to have the answer.* I literally just need to sit there and listen to what people are saying. That's what's going to help them. So, listening is the most important part of communication and it's fundamental to building you up as a person as well. Half the shit I say on the podcast, a lot of what you've read in this book and most of my values and beliefs stem from something someone else has told me. Something that resonated with an experience in my life. Because of that resonance, it stays in my mind and gets reworked into my language. I figure that by sharing it, maybe down the line it'll resonate with someone else.

The thing is, we're all learning from each other, all the time. We all go through the same shit. The situations might be different and have different scales of hardship and stakes, but fundamentally, humans are the same. That's why I love the art of communication and being able to talk to anyone from any walk of life. Every day I'm reminded that the best skill you can develop is the ability to

Every day I'm reminded that the best skill you can develop is the ability to take on advice and feedback from anyone.

take on advice and feedback from anyone. No matter what level you or the other person are at, we can all learn something from everyone. That's one of the most important ideas I've ever taken on. It's a solid bit of wisdom.

Often in my world it's Juzz who's sending it my way. Which is lucky, because she is one of the smartest people in the world. She's absolutely incredible in so many ways and has this supernatural ability to support me and cut through to me when I'm on my bullshit. Whenever she gives me advice it's somehow always the right thing at the right time, exactly the thing I need to hear in that minute, even if it's not what I'm looking for.

This one time I went to her for a bit of advice on a problem I was having. She listened and thought about it and then gave me some advice. Let's call it Solution A. So, I went away and thought about it some more and slowly it dawned on me that Solution A was a terrible idea. It would absolutely make everything worse, so I went to Juzz to complain.

'That advice you gave me? That was so shit. It was actually really terrible. Like the worst advice I've ever heard.'

'Okay,' she said. 'What did you expect from me?'

So, I thought about that . . . and told her I expected her to give me Solution B.

'Well. There's your answer then.' She smiled. And I thought, *Oh, fuck, you're right.*

She knew that I knew what to do all along and showed me that with a little Jedi mind-reversal trick. Which is really cool, first of all, and also demonstrates (yet again) that sometimes the best way to tell someone something they need to hear is just to listen to them.

Everyone has different ways that they prefer to communicate. Juzz and I know each other better than probably anyone else on the planet, but she's had to teach me how to communicate better as our relationship has evolved. Probably the same story for a lot of relationships.

Starting to do the real work

One of the most important conversations of my life is captured on audio. I'd asked Dr Zac Seidler – back before we were mates – onto the pod to talk about his work with men's mental health.[11]

I'd noticed that there was an undercurrent in all our podcast episodes of someone talking about adversity and overcoming it, or the dark struggles that they've had. And I think that kind of vulnerability, to be able to talk about that dark stuff is so important and shows real strength. So, I wanted to explore it. Until I was actually with a clinical psychologist on a hot mic. Then I wanted to be anywhere else.

Back in 2019, before recording the episode, I had never spoken about mental health or my emotions publicly. Even trying to say the words on a podcast felt weird coming out of my mouth. So my interview with Zac felt super awkward for me to record and then the thought of releasing it became a fucking nightmare. All through editing and producing, right up until it went live, I was freaking out. I thought people were going to fucking hate it and me, that people would think I was a loser. My anxiety went through the roof, worrying that no one would be able to connect with it.

I was so wrong. People loved it and Zac went on to become a recurring guest on the podcast and a close friend. Going back and listening to the episode now, I don't know what I was worried about. If you weren't me and didn't have the memory of sitting there absolutely shitting yourself with nerves then you wouldn't have any idea how stressed I was. To a casual listener of the show it probably sounds like a normal conversation, but it was a massive turning point, both for the show and me personally. After that, my chats started going beyond surface-level conversations. I really have to thank Zac for that.

'I could sense when we were doing that podcast that it was a lot for you to even just talk about the topic,' Zac told me later on. 'Once you push past that, then everything just becomes so much easier. It's practice, it's a skill.'

He wasn't wrong. I started to practise being vulnerable in my life and it was an absolute game changer.

Define vulnerable

There are several dictionary definitions of vulnerability, most of which revolve around having a weakness or susceptibility to being hurt, physically or emotionally. I prefer to define it in terms of your ability and willingness to take a risk.

In a physical sense, I was trained to make myself vulnerable as a footy player. During my career, which amounted to me collecting more injuries than goals, I was massively vulnerable. I'd get out under the lights and hurl myself at players twice my size to get the ball off them, even though I knew in the back of my mind that I was probably going to be limping off the field at the end of the day. So, physically, my ability to be vulnerable wasn't a problem. Emotional vulnerability was a different story. I was primed to harden up and be stoic and not to burst into tears when the game went the wrong way.

So, it wasn't until post footy that I learned to let my emotional guard down. The first few times I was emotionally vulnerable it was as simple as sharing that I was uncomfortable with something. Level one. Then I started to reach out of my comfort zone on the podcast, and in business, and actively putting it out there that I wanted to try or do something that I was afraid I'd get knocked down for. Surprisingly, people were there for it and gave their support. Not always, but the results were usually spectacular. That was another level.

The more I began to practise vulnerability on the podcast, it was like magic – others started opening up and some of the chats got really deep. It became one of the things that the listeners really loved about the show. Leaning into that made me a better podcaster. There are so many levels of vulnerability and exploring them was something I wanted to get better at, both for work and for personal reasons. Slowly it developed into one of my biggest strengths, without me even realising it.

But all that took time. You don't just start by turning to a stranger on a bus and unloading your biggest, darkest trauma on them. This isn't TikTok. To start, level one, it can be as simple as calling a mate and telling them you feel sad, or lonely, or worried about something. That's it. Then, just slowly build on it from there. Each time you'll find little bits to improve on, and eventually, you'll be amazed how far you can go. You don't have to jump straight in the deep end. First, learn to swim.

Not drowning, waving

Probably the rawest and most vulnerable I've ever felt is when I started sharing some stories about my family and my relationship with my old man after probably the most intense 12 months of my life. I'd been talking to Hugh and Ryan from *The Imperfects*, a podcast about vulnerability, and we'd arranged a collaborative episode where I would talk about that period in my life (which I go into a bit later in the book).

Because I was so caught up in how terrified I was about the whole thing, I didn't give any thought to the fact that people were listening in. All I could concentrate on was getting the story out without breaking down. I went into the chat using my best game-day mindset. I knew it was going to be tough, so I'd spoken to my old man before it and got his blessing.

Finally when the day came I had this huge surge of mental relief. I was ready to go and be vulnerable because the time was right. It had been a 27-year journey to get there. It was so intense in the moment, but as soon as we were done with the interview, I was stoked. I felt so good. But then . . . the week after we released it, I was the most anxious I've ever been. To this day, I haven't topped it. Looking back, I think it was just because I'd shared something I'd held in for so long, so I was just like, totally ruined physically.

I remember speaking to Juzz about it afterward and trying to explain it. 'I'm so happy I did it, and I don't regret doing it, but I'm still fucked.' It was the weirdest feeling. The closest I can compare it to is the end of the AFL season – that morning-after Monday where you've capped off months of pushing your body to the edge with a truly epic hangover. Every part of your mind and body is completely cooked, but somehow, you feel abso-bloody-lutely amazing.

As a kid, I would never have dreamed it possible that I would do something like that – be so emotionally raw, especially in public – but the response has been nothing but positive. By putting myself out there, being completely open and vulnerable with the world and sharing this hurt I'd been carrying around, I found comfort. The minute I put it out there other people started opening up to me with the burdens they'd been carrying. I realised I wasn't alone.

It was kind of a lightbulb moment for me. We think we're the only people going through shit, but the moment we make ourselves vulnerable and communicate, the universe taps us on the shoulder and goes, *Mate. You're not special. Literally everyone has shit going on in their lives.* It felt so good to finally realise that I wasn't the only person going through these issues. For so long, I thought I was. It's a shame it took almost 30 years to make that leap, but I guess how long it takes is just how long it takes.

That episode was really a catalyst for why I'm so interested in mental health and why I love having the podcast as a space to explore it. Now, I can sit around a table with my mates and openly talk about my emotions, fears, self-doubt, hopes, whatever it is. The best part is, they can do the same, because we've built that connection and avenue of communication. Making myself vulnerable and breaking the rules that say men don't share their hurt, or cry, and all that comes with that – has made my life so much richer. That was big for me. I thought I'd always had good connections with friends and family, but actively cultivating vulnerability has taken it to a whole other level.

Making myself vulnerable and breaking the rules that say men don't share their hurt, or cry, and all that comes with that – has made my life so much richer.

There's a visualisation exercise I learned from one of my chats with Zac. Imagine your mind and your emotions as a house. Inside are rooms which contain everything you need to live a good life. Your hopes and dreams and experiences and relationships. All the good shit in life. But some of it is kept behind a door you cannot bring yourself to open in front of anyone else. The stuff that your brain locks away like, *I'm keeping this out of sight forever. I don't need to tell anyone this. Nobody needs to know about it.*

But, says Zac, 'Opening up that door and leaping into that stuff, that shit's frightening. But once it opens it up, suddenly you're in a new room and you're like, "Oh my house is much bigger than I thought it was."'

It takes massive effort and practice to fight against the voice that is telling you, *Don't push that door open, it's dangerous*. But it's worth it.

The other side of vulnerability is resilience

I once worked with a coach at the Giants who used punishment as motivation to improve our game. If we missed a kick at training, we were made to do push-ups. Which basically meant, we all gave up going for kicks, because we didn't want to cop the punishment if we missed. Later, we switched up the model. Push-ups were off the menu. Once the fear of punishment was gone, we started practising our kicks again and our goal rate improved.

The same is true for emotional vulnerability. If you're afraid of the worst-case scenario, you'll never take the kind of risks you need to grow as a person. You won't go for the kicks, try the creative project, go for the dream job, ask the girl out, etc, if you're afraid of the outcome. You can still be afraid yet willing to risk it for the biscuit, knowing that you might win and that even the worst-case won't be the end of the world. If nothing else, you'll learn something.

For human beings, who are built to fear the unknown and ruminate on what could go wrong, the capacity to put yourself out there and take risks is vital to our growth. When we surrender to the uncertainty, when we just go for it, it changes our mindset. You put yourself out there emotionally and maybe the outcome is good, maybe not, but either way it *will* be okay. Vulnerability can be hard, but it can teach you incredible resilience.

Says David 'Butters' Buttifant, the man whose 'option three' got me through that cave in Tassie, 'There needs to be that element of vulnerability in us, to perceive the uncertainty of life and that we don't know what's ahead of us.'

That's how we build our resilience. When you experience that discomfort or fear, the physiological stress you're feeling, it's not fun, but it ends. Then, later, when your find yourself vulnerable again, you know you've been there before and can rise to meet it. Which is important, because there's no such thing as a 100 per cent cruisy life. Adversity is part of the package and we need to build resilience, through vulnerability, to deal with that. Because, 'If we always want comfort, we're gonna get despair,' says Butters. 'Life will give you hard choices, but easy choices will give you a harder life.'

Communication Toolkit

- The old male stereotype of being stoic, tough, unemotional and uncommunicative doesn't work in today's world. If you only give me one choice of how to be a man, that's not power, it's a straightjacket.
- Work on having 'range'. Be flexible, look at your life and the tools – the skills, talents, attribute, interests – you have and call on them when you need them. Range is about being interested in what interests you. About being real.
- Learn how to have real conversations – even if they're tough. If you come at life with the ability to have those tough conversations, everything gets better. All your relationships, how you deal with problems, conflicts, voicing need, being a better friend, sex. Everything.
- Communication isn't something we are born good at. I had to work on it and it's something I still work on all the time.

- Start small. It's important to practise with 'live ammo'. Learn to communicate even when you're feeling emotional – your heart is racing and you're choking up. If you learn to talk through tears when you're upset, you're learning a valuable life skill.
- Think of it as training for a grand final. You've probably already had a couple of emotional grand final moments in your life where you've needed to have a strong emotional muscle to handle the intensity of the moment. There's going to be more. So, think of everyday communication as training for the big day.
- More than half of communication is listening. You can't learn if you can't listen and you can't listen and talk at the same time.
- Being *interested* in people is way cooler than trying to be *interesting*.
- Communication within romantic relationships can be tricky. Everyone expresses their love differently. Me and my partner have different 'love languages' – as will 99 per cent of couples out there.
- Looking at the five love languages – physical touch, words of affirmation, acts of service, quality time and gift giving – work out which one (or several) you and your partner prefer and have a conversation about it. Don't forget to start small if you need to.

- Male-to-male banter is its own kind of communication. It's a way for us to test the boundaries and push past the superficial into real connection and vulnerability.
- Vulnerability is one of the most important skills you'll ever learn. Vulnerability means the possibility of being hurt. Which means the potential to grow. The other side of vulnerability is resilience. It's the ultimate in self-exploration, but you can only do it with other people.

FAMILY

CHAPTER 15

MY DAD

I practise gratitude every day, but probably the thing I'm most grateful for above all else is my family. My mum and my dad have been absolutely relentless in their support of me. I grew up understanding that no matter what I did they would be proud of me, and that feeling was the greatest gift a child can ever be given. It's spurred me on to push boundaries and continue keep pushing forward, make mistakes, get knocked down and get back up again. The biggest lesson they gave me went unspoken – I had to live my own life.

My dad led by example. The man has lived at least three lifetimes in 60 years. As I was growing up, every so often I'd hear bits of the legend. Stories about my dad that would filter down to me from my uncles and aunts or old footy heads down at Carlton. Honestly, I'm hoping he'll write his own book one day. The stories are unbelievable, but I can vouch for him because I saw him limp home after a few of them.

Dad was a country boy. He grew up in Kyneton, son of a hard-working butcher, alongside eight brothers and sisters. He had a good mate up that way who owned a riding school, so he spent his salad days riding horses. When the old man was a young man, he loved horses so much he dreamt of being a jockey, but when he got too big for that he had to settle for the comparatively tame world of VFL footy.

In the early 70s, he rose through the ranks of the Kyneton Tigers, playing in the Under-9s, then Under-12s, then Under-15s – all on fields so cold it snowed in the winter. So I guess that's where I get my famous country toughness from. Footy was a different game back when Dad played it, a little rougher around the edges. For example, on Saturdays for a bit of an extra challenge, and to give the locals a bit of recreation, the old Castlemaine Gaol would let the inmates out to play against the local teams.

'I don't think they'd do it now,' says Dad. 'But you'd play against some characters there.'

Dad recalls a game against one of the gaols from South Bendigo, when he kicked four goals in the first quarter. After the fourth goal, the guy he was playing on came over and grabbed Dad by the guernsey. 'Listen son,' he said. 'You go kicking another one, I'm gonna kill you.'

'I told him to go get stuffed, more or less,' says Dad with a shrug. 'Then I found out a bit after half time he was in there for murder. I sort of kept away from him after that.'

Long story short, Dad's talents stood out and he got picked up by Carlton at the age of 16 for a contract of $3000. Which, fair play, is about what I got offered for my contract with the Giants right after I'd been delisted some 40 years later. I'm all about honouring those Buckley family traditions.

Dad didn't sleep for a couple of days before his first seniors game. It was a pretty daunting task for a 16-year-old boy to go out and play against grown men in an era where on-field punch-ons and king-hits were a regular occurrence.

'Men really were men in those days,' he told me. 'I'm not saying they're not men today, but [then], if they hit you, they really hit you. You had to have your eyes about you.'

Dad's talent was extraordinary. Not the biggest or heaviest guy on the field, but easily one of the fiercest. He was a natural rover, and part of Carlton's ascendency at the end of the 70s. In 1979, in his fourth year as a senior player, Dad helped lead Carlton through a dominant season that ultimately saw them take the premiership from Collingwood. The final goal that tipped Carlton into their five-point grand final victory remains one of the most controversial and legendary events in all of VFL/AFL history.

According to the old guard at Carlton, so too were the victory celebrations. An old story goes that Dad and the boys had taken the Cup out with them while out on the town celebrating the premiership win. Dad decided that carrying it around was becoming a bit of a nuisance, so he decided to hide it. He dug a hole under the bushes of a random front lawn to hide it. The next morning he went to bring the cup back, but couldn't remember where he'd buried it.

'I don't think that was me. I get the blame for everything down there,' Dad laughed when I asked him.

Whenever there was a party, Dad was there with bells on. The first to arrive and often the last to leave, he partied the way he played, then trained the way he partied. Dad earned the nickname 'The Postman' because of his habit of getting over-refreshed and not turning up on time to events. In 1982, Dad had won the Robert Reynold's Trophy, Carlton's best and fairest award, back then. He famously got on the piss and missed the flight to Canberra and a dinner at the Lodge with Malcolm Fraser, who was Carlton's number one fan. When the Prime Minister asked to meet Jimmy Buckley and congratulate him, they had to tell him, 'Sorry, he's not here, he's posted you.'

To get an idea of what the drinking culture was around footy back then, take this one. There was a contest within the club to see who could shotgun beers the quickest. One of the boys downed 37 cans in two hours and ten minutes. 'It was a bit of a ritual for us. But we were all together and we had great fun together and we respected each other and we looked after each other on the ground,' remembers Dad. A night on the brown cordials is still very much a part of AFL culture, for better or worse, but it was a mandatory part of the bonding experience back then. 'I'd just have a beer with the boys and mingle in and all that sort of stuff. But some of us mingled a bit too early in the morning.'

This was long before AFL adopted mindfulness and meditation and psychologists to monitor player behaviour. They also had a more retro approach to injury management. Dad hurt his neck on a footy trip to Fiji when someone pushed him into the pool and he hit the bottom. In the following days his neck was playing up a bit, so the team doctor drove Dad down to the nearest city to have it checked out. The Fijian hospital had no X-ray machine, so the doctor braced Dad's neck with a towel and said, 'That's the best we can do for the moment.'

So, Dad continued with the holiday, going water skiing and playing soccer with locals, getting on the cordials. He didn't worry about it until he got back to Carlton, when he told the doctor that he had a crook neck. Dad wandered over to the Carlton clinic where they took an X-ray. The doctor took one look at the image and called an ambulance.

'Don't move,' the doctor told him. 'You've got a broken neck.'

'Jesus Christ,' my dad replied with a laugh. 'I've been running around like an idiot for the last two weeks.'

Dad was in traction for four months after that, but recovered in time to play the grand final at the end of the year. By then, though, the injuries had started racking up. The cumulative damage that footy did to his body was huge. A chronic ankle complaint saw a surgeon diagnose him with a body full of arthritis and surgeries to correct it left him favouring one leg over the other, which led to the muscles withering and throwing him off balance.

As a workaround to keep him on the field, he was getting regular cortisone injections that would offer him maybe 15 minutes of relief, until the drug wore off and the pain dropped him to the turf. As he recalls, one minute he'd be playing at 100 per cent, probably one of the most valuable players in the league, and the next he couldn't run 100 yards before he'd hit the ground. Worse, the imbalance in his body threw off his whole game.

A third surgery saw Dad go under the knife for two hours. According to the surgeon, when he pulled back the knuckle of the ankle, four floating bone shards the size and shape of lemon pips fell out – the result of a bad kick that had shattered the back of his heel long ago –and Dad had been running on it the whole time. The surgeon had never seen anything like it. After that third surgery it was another 12 months of work to rebuild his skill to anywhere near his natural level.

'It becomes very frustrating . . . it does your head in that you can't do the things you once could because your body won't let you,' Dad says, recalling his worst injuries. 'I was really down in a dark space at the time 'cause of the injuries.'

Dad versus the cordials

That headspace Dad talks about would eventually be diagnosed as depression, but when he started to suffer through it, the safety nets for that kind of thing weren't in place. Alcohol was.

Dad is a naturally friendly person. He loves going out and having a good time. For most of his life, that meant booze. Lots of it. My dad started drinking, properly drinking, at 16. He'd moved out of home in regional Victoria that year to play for Carlton, right in the middle of metro Melbourne, away from family and the community he'd grown up in. At an age where males are easily influenced, he was suddenly in an AFL environment, playing footy with grown men and partying with them too. He got swept up in all of that, and then some.

Alcohol had always been part of Dad's life. But as the years stacked up, injuries, the culture of footy, the culture of being a bloke of his generation, the part it played in his life got bigger and bigger. Which is where I come in. I couldn't tell you exactly when I realised my dad had a problem with alcohol. It's one of those things you just instinctively understand, long before you have the words for it. There's no one moment where I said to myself, *Dad drinks*, but I'd known the reality of the situation my whole life.

As a kid I'd go to a friend's house and their dad would come home from work in a suit and tie and maybe have a beer with dinner, then stop, and I would notice, 'Gee, that's different to how my dad does things.' When I was growing up, I never had friends over to the house. It just wasn't on the cards because I didn't know what sort of state my dad would be in when he got home. He might be in the best mood of his life, or he might be too far gone and ready to fall asleep on the couch.

Everywhere I went in the footy world people would tell me, 'Oh, your dad's a legend!' Which he is. But there was another side to him which only me and my family really ever saw. Dad was the most charismatic, funny, friendly, downright nicest guy you could ever hope to meet. But he also had his demons. It was hard to reconcile those two ideas of the man in my head when I was growing up.

One thing I should make clear. Even though he was troubled, he never brought it home. Dad was loving; never abusive, never physical with his family, never even raised his voice in anger. Except one time. There was one time he yelled at me and fair play, I deserved it.

In my teen years, I got home from training and went to run a hot bath to start recovery. So, I turned on the taps, got bored and left the bathroom to go upstairs and make a phone call. Nothing urgent, just wanted to call a mate and have a chat. This was in the old days, when you had the actual receiver on the phone that you had to keep nearby. Important detail, that it wasn't in the bathroom.

It must have been a good chat because I totally forgot about the bath. After an hour goes I walked downstairs, got to the bottom step and stepped in a puddle. *That's weird,* I said to myself and took another few steps to reach the light switch, into what turned out to be a bit of a lake. *Shit.*

Turns out I'd flooded the whole house. Through the entire bottom floor, the carpets were a full-on wetland. So, I started to panic a bit, trying to work out what to do. Normally Mum would know how to fix a situation like this, but she was away in Europe with my sister. So it was just me and Dad, and he was at the races, so when he came home he would have had a few beers. I remember telling myself, *This isn't good, this is not good at all*, and when Dad got home, he agreed.

He came in and looked around, then at me and sort of blinked a bit and went, '*What*?'

'Dad,' I stammered. 'Dad, Dad, Dad, don't freak out, I'm sorry.'

'I'm not mad,' he said, pretty clearly mad, but also confused. 'But WHAT THE FUCK is this!?!?'

We cleaned it all up the next day, but yeah, it wasn't good. We had to wring the carpet out. It probably set the family back a few dollars. But worst part was . . . it happened again. Four months later, I did the exact same thing. Left the bath running, chatting away on the phone, flooded the whole house and Dad came home to find it. That was a test of our relationship, but we got through it. Gee-whiz, took some time though.

Moral of the story is, nobody's perfect. Dad was living with alcoholism, I was living with anxiety and at times we both struggled with the basics, like not flooding the house twice over.

I've always been anxious, but in the years my dad's drinking was really bad, it certainly didn't help calm me down. It was a weird bit of cognitive dissonance. Because my dad had troubles and at times I was embarrassed by them, but I loved him. Everybody loves him. Dad is objectively a fucking legend. Literally, he's a legendary former player, but he's also one of the best guys on the planet.

He's so funny. Just one of the most incredibly funny cats I've met. Nobody has stories like him or knows how to tell them. Part of the reason his legacy at Carlton is so strong is because he's so charismatic and friendly and curious about people. When he's going full tilt, telling a yarn to mates, it's like watching banter-and-storytelling perfection. I look at him and he's a reflection of the things I like best about myself, only without the anxiety.

It's possible he did struggle with anxiety, which is where the drinking started. He wouldn't be the first Aussie man to self-medicate with booze. He has struggled with depression, but mental illness and alcohol abuse work together. It's a bit of a chicken and egg scenario. Which came first? We'll never know, but I watched it get worse over the years and didn't know what I was supposed to do about it. I wanted to help, but I didn't know how.

It reached its pinnacle at the start of 2021. A few things happened not that far apart that really freaked me out and I realised that something had to change. Some people on the outside had noticed Dad's behaviour escalating and had called me worried about it. He'd been able to hold it together all his life, but this was different. And maybe, with all the work I'd been doing through the pod, I was different too. *It's time*, I realised. *I have to do something to help Dad before it's too late.*

Let's get this sorted

There'd been good spurts and bad spurts over the years, but a couple of years ago, right when my media career was starting to get off the ground, things escalated. It got to the stage where Dad's love of a drink and a flutter were really starting to impact on his life. So I didn't have a choice really.

That period was a really weird time for my family. By then, Mum and Dad were no longer together. Their relationship was still really amicable, but they'd finally decided to live in different houses. This was after years of sleeping in separate beds. It was marriage breakdown and separation in super slow-motion over many, many years. At the same time my sister was pregnant and due to have a baby in two weeks, so the family had a lot going on.

Throughout my whole life until that moment, Mum had always been the problem solver in our family. She'd bailed me out of so many situations. When things went wrong, I'd just get Mum to come and fix it. That's how it had always worked. Then, with Dad's drinking escalating and her living elsewhere, I suppose I had an epiphany. *This isn't Mum's problem anymore.*

Really, it never had been. Not through lack of effort, she'd tried for so long to fix it, but it was never her problem to fix, not really. I realised if Dad was going to make any kind of change, that someone had to step up. With everyone else out, that person had to be me.

So, I picked him up one night from the pub and brought him back to my house to have a sort of intervention. Problem was, I didn't know how to do that. I just didn't have the words to start the conversation. So we ended up going back to the pub and I was just sitting with him to make sure he was safe because I couldn't do anything while he was drunk except make sure I brought him home. The next morning we went for coffee, which was unusual for us to do. And then back to his house, which is where I bit the bullet and just started fumbling through.

'Dad,' I said, 'I'm really worried about you.' I told him I knew all about his drinking and carrying on. In fairness, he took my concerns seriously, but he wasn't that worried about anything.

'Oh, don't worry about that. It'll sort itself out.'

It didn't sort itself out, but we sorted out the immediate crisis. And it was the first dent we put into the greater problem of his alcoholism. After that, though, there was so much work to do. So I started pushing for more real conversation and it was excruciating. I love my dad and our banter, but the chats we were used to having were at a fairly surface level. It was really hard at the start to try and be real and get him to let his guard down a bit. Imagine talking to your dad about this when you've waited 28 years to say something. It wasn't a dream scenario. He wasn't like, 'Oh, absolutely son, I agree I need rehab. Cool, let's sort this out.'

Basically, over weeks, I kept checking in with him all the time, trying to talk to him about his drinking and to get him to think about going to see a doctor. He kept putting it off and kept drinking until one day I realised that if I didn't *make* it happen then, something really bad *would* happen. It took probably three weeks of back and forth and other things going on for me to finally get him to agree to come and see a doctor with me, which was basically a matter of me dragging him there. 'You're going to get help, Dad. You don't have a fucking choice. We're going right now.'

I'd worked with the doctor at Carlton before, so my dad trusted him. I sat in the doctor's office while the doctor asked questions and my dad confided in him stuff I never knew or imagined.

That's when I really understood how serious the situation was. I'd never heard Dad speak about mental health and his answers were so raw. He knew that he had mental health issues, had known for a long time, but hadn't known how to deal with it. From ever since he'd been a young man. He'd actually tried to get medical help for his depression before, back when I was a kid. He'd lasted one day in treatment, couldn't handle the emotions it brought up and walked out of the clinic and into the pub. The booze helped. Until it didn't.

Dad and I came to an understanding that very slowly he would work on things and we did it together. It was a series of those really hard conversations where you sort of feel like the world's crashing around you. But I think sometimes when you have no choice but to go forward it's a hidden blessing, because you know you just have to break through. Butters' option three: just fucking get it done.

The whole time I was freaking out. That flight or fight instinct I knew from the field was firing on all cylinders, but I had to do it, so my body and mind had no choice but to rise to the occasion. At times, I couldn't believe that I was having these conversations with Dad that were just impossibly difficult.

The hardest point for me was dropping Dad off at the rehab clinic. I remember we were sitting there just crying together. That was gut-wrenching. I'd never ever seen my dad cry before. It was heart-breaking, but so special to see him finally take steps towards being vulnerable and getting better. That moment was fucking massive for me. For us, for our relationship.

A few times during this period, I'd be driving home and I'd stop at the lights and catch myself in the mirror and remind myself, *You're a fucking mad cunt. You are the toughest motherfucker in the world. You are seriously something special. How are you doing this? How do you rock up day after day?* There was just this affirmative monologue coming in, talking to myself about it, pushing myself through. It was such a shit, hard time, but in some ways it was great. It was new ground for us and we were going it alone.

No one else knew what was going on. My mum and sister had no idea. I'd pick Dad up from the rehab so we could visit my sister Jess in hospital where she'd just welcomed her baby into the world, then take him right back to rehab without telling them what was going on. They had so much on their plates already and they didn't need this to be dealing with too. I had to be the one to put Dad into rehab and be there when he got out.

Dad's been off the booze ever since, which makes me so fucking proud. Since rehab and the really fucking hard conversations it took to get him there, we've never been closer. We've never been more vulnerable. I put off that chat for my whole life because I thought it would be too hard. It was, but it wasn't impossible. The evolution in our relationship has been so good for me. There's a moment for every kid when you look at your parents and realise that they are people too, with the full range of feeling, problems and failings that anyone else has. Realising the full extent of my dad's struggles with mental health has given me more peace with my own.

If we have any good sense at all, we learn from our mistakes. But we can learn so much more from other people's mistakes. The process of being with Dad while he sought treatment for his alcoholism was so humbling – the sense of humanity and connection that came from fully grasping that we are all as imperfect as each other. We all have our own, unique struggles in life. Dad's big struggle was with depression and alcohol dependence – but the mistakes he made while on that road are mistakes I won't have to make, because he made them for me. The lessons he learned about himself are also lessons for me. That is so important.

The lessons he learned about himself are also lessons for me. That is so important.

As much as I've tried to do the best in situations, I know I haven't always made the right choices, and I understand that while Dad didn't always make the right choices either, he also was just trying his best. The hard, honest chats we had to have in order to help him with his drinking weren't easy, but the empathy they've given me is so fucking valuable. Because

I realise that we're two sides of the same coin in many ways. He has depression, I have anxiety. He's a celebrated footballer, and I've definitely celebrated football. I maybe didn't hit his heights, but I had a crack. Dad won three premiership flags. So, that's sort of one and a half between us, which is a pretty good effort on my behalf, I've got to say. Not bad at all.

The perspective I gained from going through all of that has made me realise that I truly do have the best parents in the world. I'm sometimes asked if I felt pressure to live up to Dad's legacy on the footy field. The answer is complicated. Yes, the media did speculate on that, of course they would. Let's face it, at the heart of it, away from the actual action of the game, AFL is a soap-opera and everybody loves a footy dynasty plotline. If I'm being honest, I put some pressure on myself in that direction. But I never felt it from my folks. They never missed a game, were always there to support me. They supported me when I went into footy, they supported me when I left it. Even when I first got into podcasting, which wasn't anywhere near the industry it is now, and I was just some guy talking into a microphone in a rented room above a cafe, they were proud.

'Dylan's getting into radio,' my folks would tell their friends proudly, even though I was a long way from being on the radio. That's just the kind of people they are. The best parents.

Expectations of parents

I'm reminded of what leadership and mindset mentor Ben Crowe, who worked with Ash Barty, among others, has to say about parental expectation and legacy when he came on the pod.[25]

'I get asked a lot, "What's the best piece of advice that a parent can give to their kids?"' Ben says. 'And it's the same thing I say as a coach to my athletes. It's really simple. All you have to tell them is: "I love to watch you play." Not to win the game, or kick six goals, but simply, "I love to watch you play." It shows humility and humanity and most importantly, unconditional love.'

Ben says it's easy for young people to fall into the belief that if we can't live up to the expectations or produce the results our parents want to see, then that affects their love for us. Young athletes often believe, unfortunately, that their worth is determined by how well they play. That if they play the perfect game of football, their parents will love them. So then they are caught in a trap of striving to become a perfect performer. Which, of course, is impossible.

To me, Ben says, 'The fact that you're able to have a high-profile dad who played sport at the highest levels, but you didn't get caught up in the expectations of having to follow in those footsteps for your own self-worth, is quite phenomenal.'

And that really hit home. The anxiety I felt all through AFL came from somewhere, but it wasn't from the expectations my parents put on me. Which is, as Ben says, extraordinary.

Child's play and making mistakes

Truth is, though, I don't know if they loved watching me play. It must have been super stressful for them. Because I was never the biggest guy on the field, but I certainly played like I was. Absolutely zooming into defence players at 100 miles an hour. My dad says I had no fear in me. Plenty of anxiety, yes, but very happy to break a bone if it meant moving the game along. Watching that must have been so hard for my parents. I do remember that Mum couldn't sit down the entire time she was watching me play a game. She says she wore out a pair of shoes pacing around every time I was out on the field.

My dad doesn't scare easy. He was very nonchalant about some of the close calls and capers and miscellaneous near-death experiences he's had, but the most frightened I've ever seen him was in the back of an ambulance. I got a bad hit one day in a game out at Casey Fields when an opposition player pretty much put a knee through my head. I had a bleed on the brain and a massive dent in the back of my head. For any parent to watch, that would have been terrifying.

Until recently, I didn't fully appreciate how hard it was for my parents to sit back on the sidelines and watch me take the knocks that come with growing up. Injuries on the footy field, anxiety in the playground. Gee-whiz, it must have been torture for my folks to watch me go through it and know that I had to learn the hard way. Because that's what life is all about – trying, failing, getting knocked down, getting back up, moving forward.

Because I was too young to fully understand how precious and fragile life is, and how much of your heart you put into someone else's body when you have a child, I didn't clock just how scary it was for them to watch me struggle.

I'm not even technically a father yet, but if something like a knee to the head at Casey Fields happened to my son, I would lose my fucking mind. Which is something I have to think about these days, because, by the time you read this, I'm going to be a dad.

CHAPTER 16

MY SON

Honest chat now, I'm pretty fucking stoked. I've just become a dad! (The miracles of book making; how quick did that happen?!)

I'm so excited. I'm also very scared. Because I have no idea how to be a dad, what to do, or what it will be like when I'm amongst it all. That fear is because I want to be the best dad I can possibly be. I know from talking to other young dads that part of raising a child is like any other important part of life – you just have to wing it.

At the same time, I know how important the role of being a dad is. So, yes, the whole thing has me scared shitless. But also had me bouncing off the fucking walls with joy. When I found out, my first reaction was joy. *Amazing, fantastic,*

I'm going to have a son! I am so excited to show him this life, all the beautiful things in this world. All the golf courses. I can't wait to get him into golf. It's far less stressful to watch your kid on a golf course than a footy field. The money's better too. But not long after that first wave of joy, the realisation hit. *Oh my God, I'm going to be on the other side of this fatherhood thing, having my own father–son dynamic. What the hell is that going to be like?*

The accepted idea of masculinity has changed so much from my own dad's day. I think fatherhood has a different set of expectations these days. Guys do want to be involved as fathers in the everyday stuff. Feeding and nursing and changing the nappies. I can only really speak for myself, but I can't wait to experience it all.

Go back even a few years, and the role of a dad was very different. I love my dad, and my relationship with him has never been stronger, but our own father–son dynamic, born of when I was growing up, is very different to how it would be if I'd been born today. So I don't know exactly what the relationship with my own son will look like.

Think of a role model. Someone you look up to. Doesn't matter who – could be a footy player, could be a broadcaster or muso or actor. Whatever you're into. There's a good chance they've got a story that involves them overcoming some pretty serious stuff. I myself never had a poster of Chris Judd on my wall, or Michael Jordan, or any other legendary players that I hoped to emulate one day. I just didn't have those sorts of people as a frame of reference. During my footy career, when I was asked that question, I never really had an answer.

It took me until later in life to realise that my biggest role model in life was my dad. Not because he's a footy legend, but because he's a real man who's struggled and done the hard years with his own demons. I love him, and there's so many things to love about him, but he's made mistakes. He's lived his life in a way I can take lessons from. Because even though he's got a heart of gold and he would take a bullet for me, at times he's lived a certain lifestyle and hurt people along the way. Not that he has ever done a single thing to hurt me, but honestly, once upon a time, I resented his choices.

For a while, when I was younger, I guess I saw his struggles with addiction and so forth as something I had to overcome. In time, I've come to understand that those experiences have made me stronger – I can recognise in myself that I have an addictive personality and take steps to not go down that road. It's a gift my dad gave me, through taking that path ahead of me. He's just like me – he's made mistakes in life, just like I have and will continue to do – but we learn and we work to become better men on the way.

I've gotten the impression on my journey, first through the world of elite sport and then the media space, that the shifting ideals of what it means to 'be a man' has left the new generation a bit lost. The idea of what makes a good role model is shifting as well.

For decades, the idea of role models in Australia has been tricky. Because sport is so revered in this country, star footballers are held up as these role models for kids. But they aren't always the best choice for that. No shade on anyone who's struggled, but we can all think of a sports star who's finished their career with a pocketful of cash and no direction and fallen from grace in the public eye, disappointing a lot of people who looked up to them.

I looked up to my dad for all of the obvious reasons, but I understood he was flawed as well. My mum was probably the biggest role model for me about how to be a good human. She is unstoppable, a fortress – if I had any problem in life, she would find a way to sort it out. Probably too good at sorting it out, which explains why I didn't really learn to solve my own problems until my 20s.

But not everyone can have my mum and dad in their life, as good as that would be. So, where's a young male supposed to look for healthy role models? When there are millions of young men turning to a fucking Andrew Tate for advice on how to be a man, it's clear that the role models we've inherited around masculinity are not working.

So guys without traditional role models are looking around going, *What the fuck is happening? Who am I supposed to be? What's my purpose? What's my meaning?*

I know I did. And these loud voices, that aren't necessarily the right ones, are filling the gap. Tony Robbins, Jordan Peterson, Joe Rogan – they talk with confidence and give you rules and structure, and people are hungry for that. It doesn't even matter whether these guys are speaking 100 per cent truth, they act like they are, and in doing so they're providing education, confidence and a role model, whether they're being a good one or not.

In my mind, better role models are more low-key. One of the big early role models in my life was Matt, one of my best mates' dads who coached our junior footy. He taught us a lot, about things like mateship and how important it is to look after your mates, to just be there for each other and always have each other's backs. That it's not about how many friends you have, but how many good ones. That was drilled in from such a young age and it's always served me well. A good influence at the right age, even a small one, goes a long way.

I want to be the best role model for my child that I can be. I know I'll make mistakes, like my dad before me, like his before him. But I'm going to try to lead a good example for my son in the small ways that really matter. I don't want to cast a shadow for him to grow up in, but I want to model how to be a good man, in the best way I can. Which for me means modelling vulnerability and spilling my guts and opening up space for conversations that we don't normally feel comfortable having. So here I go.

Why don't guys talk about this?

I love a chat, as you know, but this is something I find really hard to talk about and haven't spoken too much about on the podcast or any platform. For a long time, it wasn't clear whether I was ever going to be able to be a dad.

It's something I've pushed to the back of my mind because it was such a painful time. Until I finally knew that I would be accepting the role of being a dad, I really didn't feel ready to open up about it. It's a part of my story that feels wrong to try and summarise and discuss in just a few pages because it was one of, if not the most, challenging periods in my life. But I promised an honest chat here and really think this is a topic guys don't talk enough about, so let's get a bit vulnerable.

I've always wanted kids. Ever since I was a kid myself, really. When I met my partner Juzz, I started talking about starting a family very fast. Probably a little too fast – it was a good two years before we'd even decided to get married. But Juzz was keen, so we started trying, and . . . it was complicated.

Juzz and I were engaged in November 2019. But when Covid hit in March 2020, we knew a wedding was a long while off. One night, sitting on the couch, Juzz said, 'Let's just do it. Let's put the wedding planning aside and start trying for a baby.'

None of our friends were at the point of trying, they were still firmly in their party days, but we were always the first to smoke-bomb from parties and ready for life to slow down. Looking back, we are so grateful that we made the decision and were in a position to start trying 'early' – aged 27 and 28 at the time.

I really wish there was more transparency around the fact that conceiving isn't always easy. It's not how they portray it in Year 9 health class, where you're made to believe that you have sex with a girl once and she ends up pregnant. It's a real spectrum. It can take one month for some and it can take years for others. As I now know, it is considered normal to take up to a year to conceive and about 1 in 6 couples experience some difficulties with fertility.[26] Crazy!

In September that year, we found out we were pregnant – in a way that was one of the scariest moments of my life, and not at all how I imagined this news to be. I was at a party, 10 beers in, when I got a frantic call from Juzz on her way to hospital in severe pain. We soon learned that it was an ectopic pregnancy, where the embyro had implanted in the fallopian tube instead of making it to the uterus, and her tube had ruptured and caused internal bleeding. She had emergency surgery to remove her fallopian tube, and with it, we lost the pregnancy.

It was *a lot* to process. Both the surgery and its aftermath took a big toll, physically (for Juzz), and mentally and emotionally for us both. We had absolutely not been prepared for any of it. Until then, I had no idea what an ectopic pregnancy even was. It certainly wasn't something we'd ever thought would happen to us.

Once we were cleared to try again, we did, and were pregnant within the month. But not long after, Juzz was back in emergency with the same symptoms. She was diagnosed with another ectopic pregnancy. Thankfully, we caught this one a little earlier, so it could be treated with medication rather than surgery, and Juzz kept her second fallopian tube. But losing another pregnancy in this way, so soon after, was devastating.

Due to the medication we had to wait at least four months before trying again, so we tried to switch off and regroup as much as possible over Christmas and the summer break.

Statistically in Australia, the chances of an ectopic pregnancy are 1 in 100, so not as uncommon as you may think, but once you have one, the chances of having another are higher.[27] Wanting to do anything we could to avoid a third ectopic pregnancy, we decided to start IVF treatment so we could bypass the tubes all together. Although this wouldn't eliminate the chances of an ectopic pregnancy entirely, it would reduce it. We were told that, being young, we would have a great chance at successful IVF.

We were so hopeful and excited, but let me tell you, it was no run in the park. Before this, like most young guys, I had zero idea about what IVF even was. In a nutshell: it's a complex, invasive process that involves retrieving eggs from the woman's ovaries and combining them with sperm in a lab – the goal being to create healthy embryos that can be transferred back into the uterus to achieve a pregnancy and make a baby. It involves a ton of medication and hormone injections, scans, blood tests, a surgical procedure to retrieve the eggs, ejaculating into a cup in a clinic room (the most awkward thing ever), lots of waiting, and, more often than not, receiving heartbreaking phone calls to hear that things haven't worked. It's full on.

We got a positive on our first embryo transfer, but it resulted in a miscarriage. This nearly broke us. Three pregnancy losses in less than a year. This is when we really began to feel like, 'Why us? What have we done to deserve this?' Juzz was quite good about talking it through with family and friends, but for me, it wasn't something I felt I could really go into at the time. It was just all too big and all too much.

Juzz was told she had low ovarian reserve, so not as many eggs as she should. This meant she didn't respond to the treatment as well as others, so it took us a lot longer and more procedures to get any embyros to transfer. We did everything we could – followed all the advice, healthy lifestyles, did genetic testing, the works – to try and transfer only the best embryos to avoid more loss.

Throughout 2021 we experienced failure after failure. Nothing was working. We soon realised IVF wasn't a fix-all baby guarantee like it can sometimes be portrayed.

It can be hard to grasp what infertility involves until you've dealt with it personally. It's more than just about trying to have a baby, it is an unrelenting mental and emotional battle. Before our own journey I would hear about people going through infertility/IVF and felt really sorry and sad for them, but until you're in the trenches yourself you can never understand the depths of it all.

It's the biggest emotional and psychological rollercoaster. Excitement, hope, uncertainty, anxiety, fear, sadness, grief, loss, anger, denial, isolation – you feel it all. It's constantly fluctuating, intense and all consuming.

Each cycle is, give or take, a month long and comprises a number of hurdles you need to overcome to get to the next stage. It feels like you're slowly getting closer . . . but then when it fails, for whatever reason, you're shunted right back to the beginning, with no choice but to accept the situation and somehow pull yourself together to do it all over again.

During that time, every person that fell pregnant around us was a stab in the guts, and we were painfully aware of every pregnant woman or baby we saw. During lockdown Juzz and I would go for a morning walk to get a coffee and the prams would be lined up outside our regular coffee shop window. It was a constant reminder of what we didn't have. Most of the time we would sip our coffee and try to ignore them, discussing our next steps for IVF. But sometimes we would give in to it and let ourselves imagine what it would be like bringing our own pram and baby to the cafe window.

Finally, we decided we needed a break. We shifted our focus onto planning our long-delayed wedding, which ended up being the most incredible day.

We got married in January 2022, and we kept it intimate, with 27 close friends and family. We didn't want the fuss, stress or pressure of a big wedding – we'd had enough of that already and our focus was still firmly fixed on getting our baby – that was all that really mattered.

It was really special to take a pause and to realise how incredibly far our relationship had come. From two 18-year-olds who met at school, to now, the greatest team battling some serious shit together, we felt stronger and more in love than ever. It was so amazing to celebrate that. The tears were flowing as you can imagine. Going through what we had over the last 18 months made me realise how much I really wanted a family with Juzz and what an amazing mother she would become.

We continued persisting with IVF for a few more months, getting even poorer results. You just keep thinking, next time we're going to change this one thing and it's going to make all the difference, it's going to be the one, it just has to. By that point we had done seven IVF cycles and transferred five embryos, but still no baby.

We were exhausted and drained at this point, so we decided to take a break for real. Our approach to date hadn't worked, so it was time to try something new. Rest.

Everything was going so well in our lives, except this one thing, and we couldn't get out of our heads. That was when I took Ali up on his weird invitation to go to for a golf trip, and once I was there, I realised what we needed. I called Juzz and asked her to get on a plane to Europe.

'You need to get over here and have a break. We need a good holiday together, just to get out of Melbourne and out of our heads,' I said.

Juzz, who tends to be more sensible than me, pointed something out. 'You're crazy. And I don't have a passport.' Which was true, she didn't have a valid passport, and she had to be back in Melbourne in 10 days, and there were no flights available to the UK. But somehow, she got it all together. Within 24 hours she'd renewed her passport, got herself a plane ticket, and I'd flown to meet her in Greece where we had the most incredible holiday. We saw some art, some architecture. Read some great books. Ate a shitload of Greek food. Remembered to live our lives.

We returned home and found out we were pregnant 10 days later. The pregnancy was in the right place and it held. We feel so fortunate for this to have happened, and even though our son is now here, there are times when we are still in disbelief.

I wish I could say the anxiety and fear leaves you after you see the heartbeat of your baby, but it doesn't, it's something that continued fiercely throughout the pregnancy and it wasn't until we held our beautiful boy in our arms, after three years of waiting, that we could finally take a breath and feel that we had finally won. Now that he's here, I have a whole new set of anxieties and fears, but I'll save all that for another day!

While we were struggling with the fertility side of things, I felt more lost than I have in a long time. I didn't really feel like I had anyone to talk to, any research to go off, or any walls to bounce off. Which is weird for me, because normally I'm a bit of an open book. But this felt like something you don't really speak about with your mates. To be honest, I didn't want to talk about it with anyone either. It was just something I wanted to deal with myself. Which I think is fine, for some things.

Vulnerability is a choice. Even if you're in the habit of honest communication, you should only be vulnerable with things that you're comfortable sharing.

It's important to remember that vulnerability is a choice. Even if you're in the habit of honest communication, you should only be vulnerable with things that you're comfortable sharing. Because it's probably not going to serve you to talk about things if you're not ready. That whole period of struggling to conceive I really didn't want to speak to anyone, and I felt better doing that because it was all too raw and I didn't quite have the language for it.

I wasn't suppressing my feelings, but what we were going through felt so specific and personal that I didn't want to speak to anyone except my psychologist about it. Really, I didn't know how my mates were supposed to help me. I wasn't in the market for advice, because how can someone give you advice when they don't understand what you're going through?

My wife, Juzz, was the opposite. She found support in talking it through with her sister and my sister and friends. So, she loved having that support, whereas I just – I really just wanted to deal with it privately. That was a bit of a role reversal for us. Normally Juzz is very private, whereas I'm such an open book, a chronic over-sharer. But this was something I just didn't want to talk about around the dinner table, like, 'Pass the potatoes please and by the way, our fertility might be fucked.'

Why did I feel that way? With a little bit of distance, I think that I'd internalised it as a bit of a taboo subject for men. As much as I'm all about communication and go on about vulnerability and sharing hardship, this thing felt like an exception. Which is why I'm talking about it now. Because – if it was hard for *me* to do, I'm 100 per cent sure that it's tough out there for other guys who are struggling with fertility. Honestly, I didn't know where to look. I don't know of any leaders or coaches in this incredibly important area of life to turn to.

If I want to climb a mountain, or run an ultra-marathon, or help my team climb a ladder, there are people I can turn to for inspiration and advice. When it was the team of me and Juzz, though, facing down this impossible thing, I didn't know where to turn. So, I went inward. That's why I'm putting this out there, as a bit of a beacon, in case anyone wearing my old shoes feels alone. You're not.

Even if you're not going through anything like this, I feel like it's an important topic for everyone to have some understanding in because it's likely that at some point you will cross paths with someone who is and being able to keep the lines of communication open and support them, if that's what they need, is going to be a great skill to have. It's important to remember that each person struggling to conceive walks a unique path and how they'll feel and want to be supported, if at all, will be different. Unfortunately, there just isn't a one-size-fits-all guide for navigating this type of thing.

During our whole journey of trying to conceive and as I was struggling with the whole concept, I recorded a podcast with Jonah Oliver. He said something that kicked me in the face. 'Humans would rather the certainty of misery, than the misery of uncertainty.'

It was one of those bits of knowledge that just happened to hit me at exactly the right time, in exactly the right place in my mind. I felt it in my bones. While we were going through the struggle, more than anything else, we just wanted it to be over. Because we didn't know if it was going to happen, the hope that it *might* was torture. It got to the stage that if a doctor could have just told me for certain that it was never going to happen for us, it would have at least put us out of our misery. At least we'd have an answer. We could have dealt with it and moved on.

Instead, we were stuck in this torturous limbo. The closest thing I can imagine comparing it to is being told that you have a condition which the doctors aren't sure you'll recover from. You might. You might not. You don't have a timeline. Just a possibility of life going in one of two completely opposite directions. The best health professionals in the world couldn't tell us, 'You're definitely going to get there in two years, so persevere with it.' But neither could they tell us that it wasn't on the cards.

Living in that uncertainty through that whole period was so painful, but such an eye-opener. When I think about it now, I realise that it's a lesson that's set us up for life. Because, truth is, we never know what's going to happen in the future. None of us do, any of the time. It's scary, but you've just got to trust the process. This is still something I am working on today and to be honest I think I always will.

All I know out of this is how much I love Juzz. I've always loved her, but seeing what she went through and what she put her body through, how she never gave up, was genuinely inspiring. I'm not even joking – I reckon she would know how to administer a round of IVF on someone, that's how much research she was doing.

It's like most things in this book, when you think about it . . . all the special bits have come from the toughest times. Now, when I lie in bed, in the most non-creepy way possible, my favourite thing in the world to do is watch Juzz and Max sleep; 3 am vomit all down his bib, Juzz with her eye mask on, both snoring. Yeah, I'm a lucky man.

It's the craziest story that this hectic, last-minute golf trip is what led to the gift of our child, but there you go. It just reaffirms that you need to do the crazy, difficult, unlikely thing and run the risk of mistakes now and again, to finally stumble into your happiness. Nine times out of 10 those leaps don't amount to anything, but this time, it led to this. Our son. The greatest miracle you could imagine from that trip – even greater than the clutch putt Cam Smith landed on the most difficult green of the British Open.

The most important thing I ever learned

I look back now and, painful as it all was, I'm grateful. If I'd had a kid first go, I really don't think I would have coped that well with it. Maybe there's another world out there where we had a child before I was ready and ended up resenting the circumstances. If we'd started a family before I'd established my business. Or when I was struggling with my identity, or when we were having financial difficulties. Not that a child would have gotten in the way, but things definitely would have been different.

I think, because it took so much time, we've realised how badly we wanted a family. It's made us a lot more grateful for the opportunity and we appreciate it a lot more. For me, it's made me so, so grateful for my wife. I loved her before we went on this journey, but seeing what she went through to make our family happen blows me away. The level of sacrifice and courage and strength she had use to get us here. You've got no idea. Nobody who hasn't been on that journey could. She was so strong and it's made us so much stronger.

I think it's like all adversity. No one chooses it. You don't put your hands up and voluntarily shout with glee, 'Let's go through something absolutely awful.' But once you come out the other side, you may well see it as something positive. Whatever the outcome. Which for me by the way, if you hadn't guessed already, was the final goal on my list. So, result. Now I've ticked them all.

Which is timely. Because I ought to start a new list. Juzz and I have the biggest adventure possible ahead of us. It's going to be hard, and scary, and joyful, and no doubt make me cry. I'm going to make mistakes, but I'm going to be the best dad I can be, like my dad before me. Minus the cordials and the arthritis, maybe.

I can't wait to show my son this world and all the beauty in it, and to sit with him and cry while we watch *Shrek*. I can't wait for him to learn what I learned along the way and to tell him what I wish I'd known in the beginning. To tell him, *Welcome to the world, Buckley. You've got an amazing journey ahead of you. Let's go.*

Family Toolkit

- Your relationship with your family will evolve over time. Situations and experiences you looked at one way as a child will look very different as an adult.
- There's a moment for every kid when you look at your parents and realise that they are people too, with the full range of feelings, problems and failings that anyone else has.
- Good parents make mistakes. Good kids learn from them. We can take so much from other people's faults. Especially those closest to you.
- The lessons your parents learn on the way are a gift to you, to save you making the same ones.
- At some point your relationship with your parents will change from child/adult to adult/adult scenario. Those transitions aren't always easy. In the beginning you might not have the words to start the conversation. The important thing is to start.
- A role model doesn't have to be a hero or a sporting champion. All champions are flawed.
- We are all human. But we can learn from everyone we meet – their triumphs and their failures.
- Adversity is a good thing, and is an opportunity to bring family closer. Nobody puts their hand up for suffering, but working through it with your loved ones makes you stronger.

- You're never alone, even if it feels like it. That's why I'm putting this book out there, as a bit of a beacon. We might not always be blessed with the ideal situation, but family can be something you build, and with them you'll get through the tough times.

ACKNOWLEDGEMENTS

I cop a bit of flak for banging on about gratitude all the time, but seriously, I am so fucking grateful to so many people who got me to this point. Ten years ago if I'd told someone I'd be writing a book they'd probably have sent me straight from the locker room to the hospital for a concussion scan, but here we are!

Honest Chat is the result of a journey I never expected to go on, but I'm so grateful for. Every step of the way. From AFL rookie to podcaster to author. I'm as surprised as my high-school teachers probably are. None of it would have happened without the love and support of the most incredible people in the world. In no particular order:

Mum and Dad, for being the best – actually the best, number one, Brownlow-medal, Best and Fairest, Oscar-winning parents in the world. Thanks for your unconditional love and support, everything you sacrificed to give me and my sister the life we have. And for giving me the room to make my own mistakes and fuck up along the way. And especially to Mum (sorry Dad), I could write a book on how much you mean to me. I love you with all my heart and am so thankful to have had you as a parent. If I can work out how to be half the person you are, I'll be a lucky man.

Every AFL coach and player who I ever shared a field, locker room, or Mad Monday session with. I'm a better person because of your influence on my life – I've gone on to kick those goals in life that you probably would have liked to see a few more of at the MCG.

Everyone at Producey: Adam Baldwin, Zach Kangeleris, Sam Bonser, Darcy Parkinson, Scott Walton, Sam Dalton and Stefanie Winstanley, from when the business was nothing but a vague idea and an Insta handle, to the whole army today. I can't believe how lucky I am to work with all of you while we build our business. I love you all.

It may be my face there on the website, but we all know who the real credit goes to for everything we've created. I'm so grateful to each and every one of you who brings *Dyl & Friends* and the rest of our poddies to life. From research and booking guests to editing and promoting the show, you are the backbone of *Dyl & Friends* and Producey. I'm so grateful for your dedication and hard work. You are the most inspiring bunch of people and I can't believe I get to turn up and see you at work every day.

Speaking of which, I am beyond grateful for every guest on the poddy over the years. The most incredible individuals who have taken the time to sit down with me and share their stories, whether they are the greatest footy players to ever grace the MCG, or people with amazing stories of courage and resilience, or just dead-set hilarious comedians.

ACKNOWLEDGEMENTS

I have to pinch myself every day that it's literally my job to sit and talk to the most amazing people. It's been such an honour that you've taken the time to have a chat. I've learned so much from all of you, too much to go into here or the book would be twice the length it is, but the wisdom you've shared is scattered through these pages. I was never that studious, so you've got to be a truly inspiring person for something to sink into my brain. Thank you all.

Special mention goes to all the voices who are quoted in this book. Thank you so much for your permission to include your knowledge in these pages. What you told me changed my life and I truly believe everyone who hears from you will benefit from it like I have.

Big shout out to the team at Penguin Random House who took a chance on this book. My publisher Isabelle Yates, who first saw the potential in opening up a real conversation between guys, writer Liam Pieper, who made the words I said and the words you read connect seamlessly, editor Charle Malycon, who wrestled them into the book you're holding right now and the rest of the team who helped get it out into the world.

And of course, the big one, the greatest person I have ever met: my wife Juzz. I need to thank you for so many things, but your unwavering support through the hardest times is something I could never thank you enough for. You have been with me every step of the way, offering encouragement, feedback and love. I am so lucky to have you on my side.

Next to Juzz, more than pretty much anything, I'm grateful for you. The *Dyl & Friends* fam who listen to the poddy. Every single person who took a punt on the podcast – who listens, who reaches out, who makes it part of their lives. Without you, none of this would exist.

Your support, encouragement and feedback have been priceless in shaping the show into what it is today. It's incredibly humbling every time I get a message from one of you that says that when you listen to the podcast it feels like I'm your mate. I feel the same way. I'm so grateful to you, mate. Thanks for tuning in and getting amongst the chats.

I am overwhelmed with gratitude for everyone who has played a role in making *Dyl & Friends* a success. What started as a poddy is so much more than that for me. It's a community of people who share a passion for storytelling and human connection. I am so stoked for what the future holds and can't wait to continue this journey with all of you. Thank you from the bottom of my heart. Yeeuww!

NOTES

1 Worland G (host) *Man Up* original ABC TV series (2020), now available online: https://manup.org.au/tv-series/ (accessed July 2023)
2 Kaplan J, Gimbel S & Harris S, 'Neural correlates of maintaining one's political beliefs in the face of counter evidence' in *Scientific Reports* 6, Article 39598 (2016) https://www.nature.com/articles/srep39589 (accessed July 2023)
3 *Dyl & Friends* podcast, #72 Chris Judd
4 Australian Institute of Health and Welfare (2022), 'Mental health: prevalence and impact', Last updated: 10 November 2022, https://www.aihw.gov.au/reports/mental-health-services/mental-health (accessed July 2023)
5 *Dyl & Friends* podcast, #85 David Buttifant
6 *Dyl & Friends* podcast, #163 Jonah Oliver
7 *Dyl & Friends* podcast, #156 Christian O'Connell
8 *Bra Boys* (2007) Writer/Director: Sonny Aberton, Director: Macario De Souza
9 *Nanette* (2018) Writer/Performer: Hannah Gadsby, Directors: Madeleine Parry & John Olb
10 *Dyl & Friends* podcast, #108 & #176 Hunter Johnson and #123 Hunter Johnson & Zac Seidler
11 *Dyl & Friends* podcast, #37 & #54 Zac Seidler and #123 Hunter Johnson & Zac Seidler
12 Albert Camus, 'Return to Tipasa' originally published in French collection of essays, *L'Été* (1953)
13 *Dyl & Friends* podcast, #81, #128 & #177 Emma Murray
14 Hölzel B K, Carmody J, Vangel M, Congleton C, Yerramsetti S M, Gard T, Lazara S W, 'Mindfulness practice leads to increases in

regional brain gray matter density' in *Psychiatry Res.* 191(1): 36–43 (2011) https://www.ncbi.nlm.nih.gov/pmc/articles/PMC3004979/ (accessed July 2023)
15 *Dyl & Friends* podcast, #153 Samantha Gash
16 *Dyl & Friends* podcast, #79 Dylan Alcott
17 *Dyl & Friends* podcast, #166 Vinh Giang & Ali Terai
18 *Dyl & Friends* podcast, #152 Lucas Herbert
19 Sedaris D, 'Laugh, Kookaburra' in *The New Yorker* (17 August 2009)
20 *Dyl & Friends* podcast, #157 Nick Riewoldt
21 Fumitake K and Ichiro K, *The Courage to Be Disliked* (Allen & Unwin, 2017)
22 *Dyl & Friends* podcast, #120 Hugh van Cuylenburg, Ryan Shelton and Josh van Cuylenburg
23 https://theresilienceproject.com.au/
24 *Dyl & Friends* podcast, #94 Chantelle Otten
25 *Dyl & Friends* podcast, #57 Ben Crowe
26 World Health Organization (2023), '1 in 6 people globally affected by infertility', News release 4 April 2023, https://www.who.int/news/item/04-04-2023-1-in-6-people-globally-affected-by-infertility (accessed July 2023)
27 Health Direct (ND) 'Ectopic Pregnancy', https://www.healthdirect.gov.au/ectopic-pregnancy (accessed July 2023)

MENTAL HEALTH SUPPORT SERVICES

Adult

Lifeline: 13 11 14
lifeline.org.au

Suicide Call Back Service: 1300 659 467
suicidecallbackservice.org.au

Beyond Blue: 1300 224 636
beyondblue.org.au

MensLine Australia: 1300 789 978
mensline.org.au

SANE: 1800 267 263
sane.org

Youth

Kids Helpline: 1800 551 800
kidshelpline.com.au

headspace: 1800 650 890
headspace.org.au

ReachOut: au.reachout.com

Other resources

Life in Mind (suicide prevention portal):
lifeinmind.org.au

Head to Health (mental health portal): headtohealth.gov.au

ABOUT THE AUTHOR

Dylan Buckley is a former AFL footballer who played 41 games (plus many more in the twos and a couple in the twos twos) for Carlton and GWS Giants across eight seasons. He experienced the highs and lows of the game, from getting drafted to the club he grew up supporting, winning an AFL Rising Star award nomination and kicking goals on the MCG, to the struggles of injury, self-doubt and rejection (he was delisted twice).

Knowing the end of his football career was approaching, Dylan went in search of something away from the game that gave him professional purpose and the *Dyl & Friends* podcast was born. It's been downloaded more than 10 million times and features guests including Nedd Brockmann, Christian O'Connell, Richard Harris and mindset coach Emma Murray.

@dylbuckley

@dylandfriends